BUILDING THE
IMPOSSIBLE

A Refugee's Journey of Giving Back

ZEBIBA SHEKHIA

Building the Impossible: A Refugee's Journey of Giving Back

© 2019, Zebiba Shekhia. All rights reserved. No part of this publication may be reproduced or transmitted in any form or by any means, mechanical or electronic, including photocopying and recording, or by any information storage and retrieval system, without permission in writing from the author (except by a reviewer, who may quote brief passages and/or short brief video clips in a review).

Dedication

For M. Shekhia, my father

Acknowledgements

This book would not have been possible without the help of some very dedicated and wonderful people.

First, to all the mothers in the Eritrean refugee camps in the Eastern Sudan who believed in me. Your intention to get your school built was the well-spring from which I drew liberally to complete that monumental task.

To Robin Quivers. You continue to defy the odds and you embody the ability to make the impossible, possible. Your will to live gives me great inspiration, and your commitment to educating the forgotten children, both here in American inner-cities as well as in the Eritrean refugee camps in the Sudan, is commendable. Your financial support helped build the high school for girls in the Shagarab refugee camps.

To Jeff MacIntyre. You have been one of my strongest supporters, and your commitment to telling the Eritrean story—especially of the mothers in both the country and in the camps—has been a crucial element to the success of the high school. Your willingness to help the mission of Healing Bridges, (my organization to help Eritrean women and children) and your humble approach to all your work is laudable. I love your insistence on living with the truth no matter the consequences. It is a stance that we need to promote everywhere in this world.

To Lynn Rose. You have been one of my staunchest supporters throughout all the ups and downs of building the high school for girls in the Eritrean refugee camps in Eastern Sudan. Your deep, abiding love of humanity shows through in all your actions—your compassion, your honesty, your good heart, and your positive attitude. Thank you for your help when I needed it the most, and your continued support and care for my well-being and the work that I do.

To Megan G. Orlando. Your brilliant logical mind and compassionate heart assist me in discerning the deeper truths within complex situations. I trust your judgment, your keen business savvy, your legal expertise, your sisterly suggestions and wise counsel. Thanks for helping me decipher ambiguous and complicated matters rendering their meaning to me with crystal clarity. I deeply appreciate your willingness to spend time supporting me, listening to the mundane and not so mundane daily issues that arise related to Healing Bridges and me. I cherish the connection we share, and I know it is mutual and lifelong. Your devotion to my work is ever present and inspiring, and I thank you, deeply, for that.

To Beyan Negash, my brother. You are the person to whom I confide many life-related matters because I know I will always receive your honest feedback. Your work reviewing the original manuscript was key in making it coherent enough to send off to an editor, and your hard work on the final draft, making sure that all the stories were historically correct, is very much appreciated. Your critically sharp eyes and your knowledge of Eritrea and its

• Acknowledgements

people have provided me with a different perspective than mine, one I truly appreciate.

To my editor Dr. Patricia Ross. You are truly a gifted writer and editor. You "got" my story immediately, without even hardly knowing me, and you've always respected my voice. Your support and dedication to this project went beyond the call of duty. It's amazing how two dedicated souls could connect so deeply so quickly. You created an open, safe environment for me to explore my past. You helped me bring out parts of this story that I thought were long forgotten. Your insight and patience, your willingness to work with me on the book through multiple rewrites, are all wonderful gifts. I look forward to the success of all of our projects—both present and future—together.

To Yasuko Cogan. Your generosity during my illness and my treatments has been phenomenal. You have been a Godsend to me and many others, and I thank you.

To Lou Walker. Your kind heart and generosity is overwhelming. You show up when I need your help no matter how big the obstacle. Your quiet support has strengthened me in every way imaginable.

To Dr. Leo Lagasse and Anne Lagasse. Your work with Medicine for Humanity will always inspire me. You are true humanitarians. Thank you for all that you have done.

To the following I also give a warm and hearty thank you for your support with the high school for girls in the Eritrean refugee camp in the Eastern Sudan:

Jacqueline Benson, Karen Hays, Carsten Schlamovitz, Susan Ankersen, Nerida Joy, Mario Johnson, Jane Gorden, Dr. Megan Chen, Dr. Christine Collon, Erik Milosevich,

Building the Impossible: A Refugee's Journey of Giving Back

Rick Ellis, Bryan Kest, Lloyd Phillips, Beau St Clair, Craig Osterberg, Cindy Malony, Thomas Schumann, Nzazi Malonga, Maria Gonzales, (Muna, Nuru, Ametelweli, and Dahab), Zeinab Abdulwahab, Amina Adem, Omer Bakhet, Linda Kammins, Tim Dobie, Tobia Dobie, and the Dobie Family, Hadeel Reda, Colette Taber, John Lichtwardt, Carey Conley, Karine Tchakerian, David Swenson, Michline Berry, Lisa Giannini, Tristan Giannini, David Stanley, Kim Biel, Aggie Kobrin, Fatma Abeddela, Senait Abraha, Arezu Kaywanfar, Rebecca Kaywanfar, Shahram Kaywanfar, Yedvart Tchakerian, Dalia Cohen, Yosief Ghebrehiwet, Zufie Meharenna, Tesfaldet Meharenna, Saleh Younis, Genet Agonafer, Malcolm Jackson, Loren Lewis, Pam Craig, Kate Fisher, Tsega Habte, Marcy Cole, Kelly Sullivan Walden, Dana Walden, Gypsy Racco, Pilar Stella Ingargiola, Heidi Stevens, Jacqui Allen, Drusheena Kyles, Jay Here, Ardice Forrow, Sara Mata, Katherine Mewmark, Lisa Wofard, Jackie Kane, Francesca Forese, Virginia Conesa, Saula Saad, Vidar Jorgensen, Tamzyn Carra, Dina Do Couto, Sara Soulati, Duncan Rice, Gavin Pollock, Sue Wigham, Phillip Thraves, Ali Murtaza, Amal Zane, and Tamara Lehualani.

Contents

Acknowledgements v

Foreword xi

Preface xv

Prologue xix

   Chapter 1 • Freedom Lost 1

   Chapter 2 • On Being a Refugee In My
      Own Country 17

   Chapter 3 • Fleeing Towards Freedom: Out
      Of Eritrea And Into The Sudan 31

   Chapter 4 • Finally My First Taste Of Freedom 41

   Chapter 5 • America! At Last 49

   Chapter 6 • California, Here I Come! 53

   Chapter 7 • Getting Settled, Zebiba Style 61

   Chapter 8 • Eritrean Independence 89

   Chapter 9 • Finding My Purpose 97

   Chapter 10 • A Destroyed Homeland 103

   Chapter 11 • The Atrocities 107

Chapter 12 • Finding Possibilities............................111

Chapter 13 • The Astounding Truth 121

Chapter 14 • Trying to Find Bridges That Heal ... 129

Chapter 15 • You Want Me to Do What? 135

Chapter 16 • Victory … Or Defeat?.........................141

Chapter 17 • The Leader and the Minister
   of Eritrea...149

Chapter 18 • The School 161

Epilogue 167

Afterword 171

About the Author 175

References 177

Foreword

Peace is forgiveness. That, as you know, is something in which I believe firmly. Finding peace through forgiveness is sometimes difficult but always rewarding.

The struggle for that peace, along with its reward, is something you will find in the pages you are about to read. It is the story of a child of Eritrea, a small country that sits on the Red Sea. Like so many of her brothers and sisters throughout Africa, little Zebiba Shekhia had to face up to the massacre and oppression that always accompanies war. She learned how to be still when she needed, but she did not let her fear get the best of her.

Peace is also fairness, and that fairness is what this young child has always harbored in her heart. Now a grown woman, Zebiba is fighting the good fight. She wants to bring peace to her people. While this begins with the story of why she fled Eritrea, it ends with the reason why she journeyed back to her homeland, and continues to do so, not only to help those she left behind in Eritrea, but to lend a voice to a forgotten mass of humanity that fled during the Eritrean war, landed in Eastern Sudan, and then never returned.

These are the "forgotten refugees,"—that is the official label given them by the UN. They are stuck in a never-never land of lost hope. They live, as most refugees do, in unconscionable poverty. The children, if they go to school at all, are forced to stop their education early because there are no secondary schools in the entire refugee camp. So each child has been condemned to continue that life of no hope, no dreams, no possible way out. Until now.

For this story ends with Zebiba's current dream: to bring schools to the forgotten Eritrean refugees in Eastern Sudan. But it is not the end of the story of what happened to these people. That is an ongoing saga, one that will always be linked with Zebiba's work. For it is her mission to help find ways to bring peace and stability to her homeland. Zebiba has completed the First High School For Girls in the refugee camp of Eastern Sudan. She plans to continue building schools in refugee camps, giving all refugees access to education, which will ultimately give them the ability to become self-sufficient.

War is always bloody. It traumatizes, but I am always amazed at the ability of victims to forgive their tormentors. Zebiba vowed to go back, to create Healing Bridges of peace. I commend her in her mission, and I implore each and every one of you who read this book to find it in your heart how you can help. For when you help one child find his or her way out of poverty, when you give that child an education, you give that child hope. One child then teaches the next how to hope, and soon you have a people restored, a nation at peace, a world that can love.

• Foreword

My hope is that this story will touch you as it did me, so that you, too, are led to help create these healing bridges of peace with us.

God bless you all.

> Archbishop Desmond Tutu, Cape Town, South Africa 2016
> Nobel Peace Prize winner, 1984
> Gandhi Peace Prize, 2007
> Presidential Medal of Freedom, 2009

Preface

Zebiba Shekhia comes from a land far away from America—as far away geographically, emotionally, and culturally as one could possibly get. She comes from Eritrea, a small country in East Africa, bordered by the Sudan and Ethiopia.

Its long coast line on the Red Sea has made it ideal for colonization. Eritrea has been occupied by almost everyone, from the Turks, Egyptians, Italians, and English, to most recently its neighbor, the Ethiopians. It is because of Ethiopia's colonization that she had to flee her village and tribe, and make the long journey to America.

Invasion of one country by another is never peaceful; it is a bloody, suppressive affair with families torn apart and ways of life destroyed. When the Ethiopian soldiers raided her village, she lost the peacefulness of her birthplace, the beauty of her beloved Eritrean lowlands, and the security of tribal traditions that sadly no longer exist.

Who knows what would have happened to Zebiba if she were still living in Eritrea. She is very independent, and while a highly regarded trait in the United States, it is something of a liability in Eritrea. However Zebiba told me, she's not one for "what ifs," and is grateful her life has been rich, sometimes turbulent, but always a beautiful adventure.

She wants us to share in these adventures in order to learn more about what's happened in this tiny country, half a world away. The Eritrean Freedom Fighters were finally successful in liberating Eritrea after thirty years of war, but rebuilding a country from a colonial past is almost as difficult as the colonization itself. There are always clashes of ideas and ideologies and often the average citizen is caught in the middle of sometimes violent and contentious politics.

Right now in Eritrea, Zebiba's countrymen and women are starving, and not just for food. Many women were widowed and have children who need food and clothing and who also need an education.

Zebiba has always been driven to help those in need. Here in America, she is able to fulfill her mission: to continue to build schools to help Eritrean refugee mothers and their children.

Zebiba will never surrender to the despair or abyss she has witnessed too often in our world. Hers is an indomitable spirit. God gives us what we can bear and no more. What she has borne through her life is more than most, but that has only made her stronger. Her hope, always, is that her work can help bring back freedom and openness, not only to those in Eritrea, but to the world.

As she continues to help the refugee mothers and their children, especially those in the forgotten camps, I also hope those here in America who support Zebiba's humanitarian work will become revitalized in their knowledge of how precious our freedom and individual expression really is.

• Preface

This is Zebiba's story. I hope it will touch you, so you, too, are inspired to build the many healing bridges of peace that Zebiba must continually cross.

Jeff MacIntyre
Emmy-Winning Producer
Owner, Content Media Group

Prologue

The Camp

I didn't want to go back. I was too afraid of what I'd find. But I willed myself to get in the car that morning. I had a job to do. I needed to talk to the mothers. I had to know what *they* wanted.

It had been thirty years since I had seen the camps. I never stayed in them, but I knew them well. I was warned not to stand out too much.

What I saw shocked me to my core. The tents were ratty, dirty rags, the letters U and N barely perceptible on the sides. People milled about everywhere and watched, distrust apparent in every aspect of their stance towards me.

My years in America changed me. I attracted notice, even though I was wearing the traditional white muslin robes of my countrywomen. I could feel my heart starting to break from the weight.

I willed myself to take one step, then another. I said "hello" in my native dialect, but it sounded foreign, even to me. I searched out the women and got to work.

"I am here to help, what do you need?" I asked over and over. People were unwilling or even afraid to talk to me. I learned that many well-meaning people had come to the camps promising to help—and they would bring water or food, for a while. But the camps are so remote, and it is extremely difficult—almost impossible actually—to get anything done in them. I thought to myself many times, "Now I know why these are called the forgotten refugees by the U.N."

The refugees were also, at first, unsure of my intentions. They were used to the Eritrean military, representatives of the government, kidnapping their children and conscripting them into the army. I knew about the state-sanctioned abductions. Word had gotten out about what Isaias Afwerki, leader of the Eritrean People's Liberation Front (the EPLF) and now "president" of Eritrea, was doing. He ordered the boys "conscripted" from the camps because the pool of young people in Eritrea was practically non-existent. But pretty much everyone knew that the real reason was he wanted to keep the refugees from rising up, and he needed to ensure the strong young men were working for him, not against him.

I was determined to help the mothers, so I carried on. "I am here to help. What do you need," I asked again. And again. Word spread of what I was doing. Mothers started coming up to me: "We want a high school for our girls."

I couldn't quite believe what I was hearing. The refugees have no consistent supply of food or water. Sanitation is almost non-existent. I kept asking them about it, but they were firm.

They wanted their girls to be educated.

I didn't say "Yes." I did *not* want to promise them something I could not deliver. Instead I said. "I will do my best."

• Prologue

"Try isn't good enough" their eyes told me. I knew why. They had been promised so much by so many—but nothing had changed.

I knew what I would be up against. Everyone feared for those who remained in our homeland. At the time, my oldest brother was the Eritrean Minister of Health. He warned me continually about what I could and could not do. That I was able to even get to the camps was practically a miracle.

I made a vow to myself. I would find a way to get that high school built. I was betting my life, literally, to give those girls the education they desperately needed.

But I also realized those brave mothers knew exactly what they were doing. An educated daughter would have far better opportunities in life. An education was their ticket out. And even though I was with them only a short time, I fell in love with those refugee girls and cared for them as if they were my own. I saw myself in them, and I knew I needed to help them no matter what obstacles were thrown my way.

To keep that vow required everything I had, including my health. It took me to the darkest depths of depression, for when I returned home, I felt *utterly* defeated. The dauntless, defiant woman I had become was broken, lost in a sea of despair for the refugees. I fought it, tried to keep going, but in the darkest moment of my life, I felt like I couldn't keep my promise. It made me deathly ill. One of the last thoughts I remembered before I went unconscious was that at least death would end the constant nightmare of the faces of those women haunting me, hoping against all odds, that I could keep my promise.

I didn't die then. I was in a coma for several days, but when I regained consciousness, my lungs were irreparably damaged. However, I figured that since I was given this reprieve, I better find the courage to live and make good on that promise.

So that's what I did. Barely able to breathe, I wondered how I would do it all—change the mindset of those in charge of the camps, find the money, convince a non-profit to do the work. The task ahead seemed completely, overwhelmingly, impossible.

I knew that if I was ever to keep my promise to those mothers, I would have to summon something from the deepest part of me—something that came from my core, the steel that was forged as a young, curious girl in the Eritrean lowlands.

CHAPTER 1

Freedom Lost

When I was about nine years old, my mother bought me my first pair of shoes. As a child of the lowlands of Eritrea, I spent my life up to this point blissfully barefoot. The only other shoes I had ever worn were flip-flops during the rainy season. We had just recently arrived in the city of Asmara because my family had to flee my village, Tekreret. The Ethiopian soldier's raids had gotten so bad we feared we wouldn't survive the next one.

So here I was, a war-refugee basically, living with my extended family in a city that was unappealing to my senses and uninviting to my spirit.

To make matters worse, the shoes I was being forced to wear were ***ugly***. They were an insult to all of my senses. They suffocated my feet, and they represented all that I disliked about my new surroundings. But I was a resourceful child, and my cousin had something we didn't normally get in my village—fingernail polish! I couldn't wait to get my hands on this wonderful stuff. Brandishing the brush, I dabbed every inch of my city shoes with flowers, butterflies, anything that reminded me of the freedom of my village life.

If my feet were suffocating, at least they'd be wrapped in something beautiful.

My cousin was enchanted. My mother was appalled. "Do you realize how much those shoes cost?" she scolded. It didn't matter. Those shoes, now emblazoned with color and nature meant that I could look down and remember, remember where I had come from and how far I had traveled. Little did I know how far I had yet to go.

...

I was born in the early 1960s. Tekreret is a very small village in the lowlands of Eritrea, Africa. When I was young, my world was magical. I lived the life of a tribal child (albeit not willingly), blissfully unaware of the political storm that was about to hit my homeland.

When I was a child, I didn't know that Eritrea wasn't actually a sovereign nation. It had been "federated" to Ethiopia by the U.N. in the 1950s at the height of the cold war. It was done as a conciliatory gesture as a way to appease Eritrean aspirations for independence (it had been an Italian colony since 1890) and reconcile Ethiopia's desire for sovereignty. It didn't work—because the very nature of a "federated state" means that the subordinate country has transferred a portion of its sovereign power to another. When I was a baby, Haile Selassie, the crowned Ethiopian Emperor and despotic dictator, dissolved the federation and started the process of taking over Eritrea.

Before the Ethiopian invasion, Tekreret was a beautiful location with both desert and jungle environments. We lived simply. We had our own hut, which we used mainly for

Chapter 1 • Freedom Lost

cooking and storage, and animals were everywhere. Except during the rainy season, we slept outside on beds made of wood and rope. I remember how wonderful it was to just look up and feel like I could touch the stars.

My childhood was a place full of color and movement, bright light and unfettered air. My favorite thing to do was to run home from school, lie on the ground, and look up into the sky through the huge banana and palm trees. These trees not only gave us color but some necessary respite from the hot air. For it was always hot, constantly hot. But I don't remember the heat so much as the air. I miss the air still to this day. It was always in constant motion, but it was clear, so clear that you could feel the freedom of the birds as they flew through it, whistling away into the limitless sky. Because there were no buildings or cars to block the wind, you could hear the complex whispers of its soft rush through the palm trees. Their huge fronds would create waves, much like the Pacific's waves as they come into the shore on the Santa Monica pier, one of my favorite places in my adopted home in America.

Within my soul, I can still feel those days long ago like they were only yesterday. They are with me everywhere I go, hiking in nature or walking anywhere along the coast of California.

Not long ago, I went to a friend's house in Topanga, a canyon north of Santa Monica. He had a bed outside since it was summertime. I laid out there in the hot wind and that took me back to those beautiful times in my village. In that haze between wakefulness and sleep, I was transported back to when I used to sleep outdoors under the naked moon and stars. There were so many stars in that African sky; it was like looking into a profusion of light. It wasn't harsh, just millions and millions of bright points that gave me peace.

My village was also a place of simplicity, as most tribal communities are. We didn't have insurance, for example, but what we did have was intuition. The people are strong both physically and spiritually. And we are open and honest. We don't hide our shortcomings; they are simply a part of who we are. Anyone who travels to the lowlands of Eritrea remarks on this openness. We also help each other. We are a community-oriented culture and because of that, we create bonds as strong with each other as we do with the land itself. My first years were spent in a world where relationships were measured not by what material things were given, but by what that person could contribute to you spiritually. I have brought this intuition and strength with me on my journey, and it is something for which I am profoundly grateful.

Like any tribal community, however, it was not all exotic. It was also a world heavy with tradition. Men and women had clearly defined roles. Girls were relegated to "woman's work," cleaning, cooking, and caring for the children. After school, for example, boys would go off and play soccer, but the girls had to stay home, make their brother's beds and then get ready for dinner. I didn't like that part. I actually often rebelled and didn't do what I was supposed to do, but it was part of my world, nonetheless.

The other dominant feature in my childhood landscape was the camel. I vividly remember camels and their owners walking through the village trading goods. The camel is an amazing animal, intelligent, gentle, and beautifully graceful to watch. They really can travel for long periods without

Chapter 1 • Freedom Lost

water because when they drink, they accompany it, literally, with buckets of salt. They would scoop large quantities of salt on their long tongues just like it was ice-cream, and then drink water out of the same bucket. Because of their stamina, camels played a crucial role in the Eritrean struggle for independence, and it is why the camel is on Eritrea's currencies and other important emblems that one finds enshrined on various important public insignia. It was on a camel that I fled Eritrea.

There are numerous songs and works of art, by many artists, dedicated to the camel. The Eritrean appreciation of a camel is endless, but I remember the camel in its more humble functions. In my village, the camel man and his steed were the grocery store and mall all wrapped into one. He would bring vegetables and chickens, just like I see the mail carriers delivering letters here in the U.S.

The whole economic system, actually, was dependent on that wonderful beast. On a daily basis, people from the countryside would have their camel carry various goods to sell, everything from wood for cooking, milk for daily consumption, and tea and sugar for our daily ceremony (our version of the Spanish/Mexican "siesta").

These tradesmen would take these goods into the city, sell them, and in return buy those things that only the city could provide: highland spices and grains that were finer because they were more processed.

From a small girl's point-of-view, I found this huge creature a work of art. When the tradesmen brought their camels to sell their goods, I could feel the peacefulness of these wonderful creatures, the elegant way in which they walked, the artistic style in which the camel man whistled and spoke to his camels to sit with huge piles of goods upon their backs.

I was always fascinated by the meticulous way in which the camel seamlessly folded its legs so as to not cause any damage to the things that it carried. I swear the camel knew that what it carried was fragile compared to its great weight. I remember thinking that when the camel went through its graceful process of sitting down, it looked like a mountain was coming down to its knees just for me so that I could see its fascinating hump.

When my mother married my father, she moved to Tekreret. She thought it was a permanent arrangement. It wasn't an easy move for her. She was a city girl from the highlands with social, ethnic, and cultural mores far different than that of my father and the lowland culture. She also spoke a different language than my father. My father spoke Tigre, the language of the lowlands, of the country. My mother spoke Tigrinya, the language of the highlands, of the city. Tigre is a very mellow and soothing language; Tigrinya is harder on the ear.

My mother had an especially hard time adjusting to life in Tekreret. On one occasion, she meant to place an order for chicken. Her intent was to say, "I would like to buy thirty cents worth of food." Instead, Mom told the camel vendor, "I'd like you to buy me for thirty cents."

The next day, the camel man came and tried to hand my father thirty cents. He said something to the effect of, "I'd like to buy that woman, the city girl, for thirty cents."

My father who heard this partly in shock and partly in confusion said to the man, "That's my wife from the city! What on earth are you talking about?"

Chapter 1 • Freedom Lost

Sensing erroneously that my father was bargaining hard, the camel man responded in all seriousness: "Okay, I'll buy her for thirty cents more, but remember, she's only a city girl!" I'm sure my mother was mortified when she found out what she had said, but it didn't stop her from using her new language.

They obviously adjusted, because I came along and then my younger brother. I can't tell you exactly how long my parents were married when I was conceived. Like most tribal cultures, dates, incidents, occasions, childbirth, and the like are related through events, not dates.

For example, if I were to ask my parents when they were born, instead of telling me the date, they would simply say, "oh, it was when the Italians were ruling Eritrea." But Eritrea was colonized by Italians for almost sixty years. How does one narrow down the date?

Sometimes, a person would get more specific and say, "Oh, it was about five years before the English came to rule." But this was not the norm, and the normal curiosity of a young person gets easily squashed with such vague answers that meander around without ever getting to the exact truth. Even though I have no birthday that I care to celebrate, I know it's safe to say that as I write this, those first Tekreret nights of my childhood, so peaceful and free, were around fifty-five years ago. In a way, I'm glad I don't know my age exactly; I have enough of an idea and that is fine.

I was very fortunate. Both my mother and father were very free spirits, and they allowed me to explore my world in a way that didn't always fit with tradition. Even though my culture dictated that I should stay at home after school and help my mother with household chores, I told my mother that I didn't want to do them. I wanted to be outside, exploring the world as boys were allowed to do.

I remember once when my mother wanted me to do chores. I told her, adamantly, that I didn't need to learn how to do that because I was going to move to America. She still tried to make me do it, but I just tossed back my head like a defiant colt and walked away. My mother was shocked, as she often was with me, and I remember looking at my father who wore a surreptitious half smile. He liked my spunk, my dad.

While my mother taught me to be resourceful, my father was the key figure who helped to cultivate my great sense of independence. I was his first-born, and he took me everywhere with him. It didn't matter to him that I was a girl, not a boy, which is preferred in my culture. The neighbors all commented, "He's just raising her like a boy." My Dad never stopped to listen, and I paid no attention. We would just be off on adventures as often as possible.

He allowed me to question my world, something girls weren't supposed to do. He also used to let me experience the male world. He used to take me to camel races, for example, simply because I wanted to go. Camel races were frequent in my village; along with soccer, the races were the main form of entertainment. I loved watching the camels run. Camels move so majestically, without force. They are very gentle animals when they are in service, but, in a race, these huge creatures transform themselves with such ease that one can't help but wonder where all that force is preserved. It is an amazing sight. When they are racing each other, camels *glide*. A cloud of sand fans out on either side of them as they run, and the desert, which normally

Chapter 1 • Freedom Lost

can muffle any sound, roars with thunder. I just itched to climb aboard.

After the men proved their prowess on a camel, the boys were allowed to race. I asked my father once if he would let me. He did! I didn't know what I was doing, and when the camel first took off, it literally took my breath away. It really did feel like the first part of a free fall from an airplane or a bungee jump. The best part about it, though, was that I won! I beat all the village boys, even though I had never been on a camel before. This, of course, drove the boys crazy. They didn't like me much anyway because I was always fighting them. We would get in fist-fights because they didn't like that I wasn't doing "girl" stuff. I learned how to hold my own against those boys.

To get my school built, I reflected at one point, I would still have to fight the village boys, but this time I knew I had to use diplomacy instead of fists. I wondered if what I had learned from my dad had prepared me enough to win that fight.

There was one tradition, however, that I could not run away from or ignore, no matter how hard I tried. Around the time that I was racing camels, it became my time for the female rite of passage that is common in many African countries. I had to endure the procedure for female circumcision. My mother had actually waited to have it done because she knew how badly it would affect me. When other girls had it done, there would be a ceremony performed around the whole procedure and all the village women and their daughters would attend—all except me. I refused to attend any circumcision ceremony, and once a ceremony was completed, I wouldn't talk to the girl or to her mother

9

for a while. I wouldn't even go near the place where it was performed. I even told my mother that if she ever did that to me, I would never speak to her again.

Female circumcision is a firmly held tradition in Africa, and my mom was getting a lot of condemnation from everyone because she hadn't put me through the procedure. She decided that it was my time, but when it happened, I refused to have the ceremony. I was adamant. Ceremonies are for celebration, not for pain. My mother also made sure that the procedure would be minimal. While I was cut, I was not sewn up. The whole experience was beyond painful; I was fortunate, however, that mine healed quickly. Some girls lose their lives to infection.

After it was over, I looked at the whole experience and decided that I did not like how powerless it made me feel. The whole operation was such a violation, and it took so much away from me. I was no longer able to race camels. It was physically impossible for a while. But, it was something more. Before the cut, I never once considered that I couldn't do something because I was a girl. Before the circumcision, I never felt weak. The boys used to say, "Don't mess with her. She'll kick your butt." Afterward, that all changed. I never, ever wanted to feel that I couldn't take care of myself. But after the whole ordeal, I felt weak, not just physically but spiritually and emotionally.

Even though I was demoralized, I wasn't beaten. I vowed that if I had a daughter, I would never do that to her. I also knew that I had to find some way to educate women of my generation so that the whole procedure would cease to have any cultural influence. The whole thing also seemed illogical. Why would God give us something that we wouldn't

Chapter 1 • Freedom Lost

ultimately need? If a body part wasn't needed, we wouldn't have it, so therefore, is it necessary to cut it off? I'm sure that if I were able to sit down and talk with my father about it, he would have agreed with me.

The cultural forces that keep women subordinated are strong in the lowlands, but with the help of my father and others, I was able to grow up with the idea that what I thought mattered. One of these other people that had a huge impact on my life was one of my teachers, *Sthad* Adam. I learned a tremendous amount from him. The term *Sthad* is a very highly regarded way to address a teacher in my country, and *Sthad* Adam was like my father. He didn't treat me like a "girl." I was always full of questions. I wanted to know why I was learning a particular subject, or why *Sthad* Adam spoke different languages. Instead of ignoring me, he would look me in the eye, something that, again, was just not done, and answer all of my questions. I was especially keen for him to teach me English.

I was always after him: "You come from the city, why can't you teach us English?"

He would admonish me: "When are you going to give up that crazy idea?"

I was probably around four or five when the first raids on our village started. Selassie had is eye on the great prize of Eritrea, the long coastline of the Red Sea. The name "Eritrea" is actually derived from the Greek word for "red" and the Red Sea was once called the *Erythræan Sea*. Just like the Italians and the Ottoman Turks before them, Selassie saw the vast trading opportunities afforded by that long coast.

What it came down to for me was that people who we thought were our neighbors and friends, the Ethiopians (in reality the Ethiopian soldiers), were determined to own everything about us—our land, our minds, and our hearts. They underestimated our spirit.

When the U.N. federated Eritrea to Ethiopia, it was supposed to last about ten years. The Ethiopian government never honored this agreement. Once Selassie took over, he wasted no time in degrading and oppressing us. His first act, for example, was to systematically strip Eritrea's official languages, Tigrinya and Arabic, that were used in educational systems throughout Eritrea as well as in city governments. Then, after Selassie dissolved the Eritrean parliament in 1962, a group of Eritreans had had enough. They formed a band of Freedom Fighters dedicated to winning Eritrean liberty from the Ethiopian government. These Freedom Fighters have become practically mythic—and rightly so; their heroics and eventual victory over the Ethiopian communists is now legendary, especially throughout Africa.

While most of the Freedom Fighters deserve all the honor and respect we give them, not all of them had Eritrea's best interests at heart. Unfortunately, revolutionaries never make good rulers—as evinced by African dictator after tyrannical, suppressive dictator. As the continent freed itself from the shackles of European colonialism time and again, these newly independent countries would find themselves in the grips of ever worsening violence and the egregious despotic misuse of a ruler's power. Eritrea sadly ended up no differently. But I wouldn't know that for many, many years. Growing up, *all* the Freedom Fighters were my heroes.

War came to my village long before it affected the other areas of Eritrea because the Freedom Fighters found that they were most effective when hiding in the lowlands. In

Chapter 1 • Freedom Lost

response to this planned aggressive take-back of our independence, the Ethiopian military began raiding our villages to quell the rebellion. Haile Selassie was a brutal man and his soldiers did his brutal and bloody work. Since the majority of our Freedom Fighters hid in the lowland villages, we became the primary targets of the Ethiopian soldiers. For several years, the villages around us were raided. Horrifying stories would come to us from the surviving villagers. Murder was everywhere.

Since I was fairly young, I was especially affected by the story of Ethiopian soldiers murdering the father, mother, and older children in a family so that the younger children who were left would either perish, or they would grow up with weaker ties to their tribe. While I was frightened by this, I knew, like everyone else, that sooner or later raids would take place in our village. They started when I was about six, and for three years until we finally fled, Tekreret was raided and attacked about every six months.

I do not like to dwell on the horror of those raids. Instead, I think of how we survived. The only way we knew the soldiers were coming were the cars. Cars rarely came to our village, but that is how the soldiers traveled. They would jump out when they got close to the village and just start killing people. We always knew what to do when the soldiers came; everyone living in those villages knew. There were two choices. The first was run—just run—and never stop. We didn't run to a specific location, mind you; we just ran around and around until a safe harbor could be found. Usually this meant finding one's parents or neighbors.

As children, we thought if we kept running, there was a chance we could escape being cut. You see, the Ethiopian soldiers didn't use guns. They preferred to use their machetes and bare hands. They would just cut people left and right. The second choice we had was to just lie on the ground like we were dead. There were many times when I was rolled tight into a human ball, practically biting my own knees so I wouldn't scream with terror. To shut out the screams of people being massacred, I would go over in my head, "There has to be a better life than this. There just has to be something better than this." That better life I was calling for I eventually found in America, but at that moment, fearing for my life, the only thing I could do was to think of something as far away from that moment as my young mind would allow me to imagine.

The Ethiopian soldiers were relentless. If they saw any two-legged creature move, it would be the end for that person. For that matter, many four legged creatures, especially the dogs, were also victims of the monarch's troops. During the night, if they sensed any movement, the soldiers would just shoot. It was common to wake up and see dogs lying dead on the streets. Imagine living in a world where murder was the fate of any creature that moved, especially during the dark hours.

Each time after the soldiers left, those of us who survived the raid would survey the damage. We would care for the wounded first. Most huts were burned and destroyed, and there were always many dead bodies. We would bury them, and the surviving children sometimes participated in burying the corpses of their parents. We would then move on and prepare for the next attack. That's just how it was.

The attacks persisted unabated, year after year. As I grew older, I became more aware of the horror of what was

Chapter 1 • Freedom Lost

actually happening. Even though the adults tried to keep a semblance of "normal," I noticed that the children were being targeted more and more. In actual fact, the Ethiopian soldiers had a standing order to target the children. It was their way of effecting genocide on the population—kill the next generation. Not only would that paralyze the parents with grief, it would also take care of the Ethiopian government having to deal with future problems.

I remember vividly the incident that prompted my mother to declare we were leaving. It was gruesome and involved a pregnant mother. Even though this wasn't the first time something like that happened, my mother had had enough. Even though once the Ethiopian solders did their bloody work, they would leave us alone until the next raid, she insisted we leave that night for Asmara.

It is interesting, actually, thinking back to that night we left. I don't remember any of the details. It is like I fell asleep and didn't wake up until we got to the capital city. I do have vague memories of it all happening very fast, and I was very afraid that we would never come back again. I had been to Asmara on a number of occasions to visit my grandparents and other extended family members, but we had always returned home. But this was no ordinary move. It happened with an aura of danger that loomed ahead, a danger that could easily take any of our lives and over which we had no control.

When I fled Eritrea for good in 1978, we travelled through Tekreret. Since then I have visited my beloved village twice, and unless the political situation changes drastically, I will never be able to step foot there again. But no matter if I can be there or not, it's a place I cherish, even in my darkest hours. I can feel the wind and see the bright stars in the big night sky. I am sure they are still there, beautiful as ever.

While it is my homeland, the place of my heart, however, it is not my home. Too much has happened to me and to Eritrea. But this doesn't stop me from constantly searching for ways to recapture the beauty that is still there.

I may not paint my shoes anymore, but I have certainly found ways to paint my life in a way that honors what was best about Tekreret. For that I am grateful.

CHAPTER 2

On Being a Refugee in My Own Country

By the time we fled Tekreret, the infrastructure of Eritrea was dismantled. The roads and bridges were destroyed so the soldiers would have a more difficult time getting around the country.

The jungles were also gone; the trees were cut down or bombed so that no one would have any place to hide. So a journey that would usually last one day by bus or truck seemed to take forever because we were constantly being stopped. We were in constant danger of being discovered as we traveled. We really didn't know if we would make it to the capital city alive.

Because my mom was from Asmara, we had an excuse to be traveling. We were lucky. Most of the people, my friends and their families, couldn't leave the village and the raids because they had no reason to be traveling and would have been killed by the Ethiopian soldiers. Even with my mother's "excuse," the journey was still treacherous.

Because of all of the uncertainty of who was "civilian" and who was "Freedom Fighter," the Ethiopian soldiers were very suspicious of anyone wanting to enter or leave the city and had tight restrictions on travel. To them, anyone who entered the city could be a possible Freedom Fighter, and anyone who wanted to leave was a Freedom Fighter in the making.

Not only were the Ethiopian soldiers overly suspicious of anyone traveling, they were also overly nervous because they suffered from a language deficit. The soldiers couldn't speak the Eritrean languages. However, that wasn't the case for the Eritrean Freedom Fighters. When Haile Selassie took control of the government, he forced the school system to convert to the official language of Ethiopia. Taking away one's national language is demoralizing, but it turned out to be a benefit for our Freedom Fighters. Because the Freedom Fighters could speak the Ethiopian language, they were able to infiltrate the Ethiopian military garrisons and gather intelligence information. Because the Ethiopian soldiers rarely spoke Tigrinya (our main language), they didn't have any intelligence information. This made them even more neurotic over who was "safe" and who was a freedom-fighter "enemy." We were all too aware that they often simply assumed that everyone was the "enemy," and they were under orders to kill all "enemies."

To top it all off, at this point in the war, the Ethiopian military was vigilantly protecting the capital from clandestine operations conducted bravely by the Freedom Fighters who were becoming increasingly bold in committing targeted killings of Ethiopian officials in Asmara and the surrounding areas. Against such a tense and tenuous backdrop, even with our good "reason" for coming to Asmara to visit relatives, it was still incredibly difficult to travel from one region of Eritrea to another.

Chapter 2 • On Being a Refugee in My Own Country

In spite of all the dangers, we finally made it to the capital. As I said earlier, I really can't remember the details of our journey other than feeling extremely afraid. I think that after what I had just witnessed in my village, I was in shock and my young mind had had enough. It was simply blocking out all stimuli during our trip. When we got to Asmara, my mother's parents welcomed my father, mother, my youngest brother, and me. But as I learned quickly, that welcome did not extend from the city itself.

I was definitely a refugee, an outsider, to this new way of life. My village life had been carefree: wide open fields, running around barefoot, sleeping beneath the stars. From the very beginning, I felt as if everything in the city was closing in on me. Where we ate was confined, where I played was restricted, even where we walked seemed limited. I had to sit straight up, with knees together, and I had to eat the "correct" part of a chicken.

In retrospect, it is kind of funny to think about. In the highland culture where I was suddenly dumped, chicken parts are relegated to the children based on age. For example, the older ones were allowed the meaty parts, the thighs and breast, while the youngest ones were given the wings. At any rate, back in Tekreret, I could sit "Indian style," and it didn't matter if I or my dog ate the chicken breast or the thigh. It soured my appetite for chicken.

In the city, there were no huts with refreshing spaces in between, just endless miles of boxes stacked and compressed upon each other, where everyone lived, it seemed, stacked and compressed lives. Especially annoying to me were the miles and miles of concrete. You just can't lie down on concrete and watch the clouds and palm trees; it is too cold and hard, uninviting, really, just as the city is.

I longed for my palm trees and warm earth, for the constant breeze that cleaned the air.

Although there were no paved roads in Tekreret and the floors of the huts were made of dirt, it never felt dirty to me. Dirt has a wonderful fresh and fecund smell, but the city smelled dirty, nasty even, with car exhaust and too many humans packed too closely together. And finally, there was the noise. Automobiles, buses, donkeys, horses, and endless chatter, it was just a commotion that I could not bear to listen to on a daily basis. If this was modernity, I wanted nothing to do with it.

Because the Freedom Fighters were still primarily located in the lowland and had only begun to fight in Asmara, sneaking in and out quickly to kill an official here and there, Ethiopian soldiers had not yet started large-scale raids in the large cities. The city dwellers, especially kids my age, seemed to be oblivious to what was going on in the lowlands.

Most of the adults in Asmara knew of the village raids, the escalating violence from the Ethiopian soldiers, and the increasing massacres. While they all related to our plight with sympathy, no-one in the city made the emotional connection to the murders and village raids that my family and I had lived through. But every person living in Asmara knew in their hearts that the same violence would eventually reach each of them.

Asmara seemed so modern that I couldn't quite comprehend that this city was in Africa. There was some logic to my confusion. The Italians who built the city when they colonized the country attempted to model it after their capital city, Rome. Asmara is actually often referred to as little Roma or *Bella Asmara*. Indeed, there are boulevards with neatly designed sidewalks and streets to match, and the Italians built a beautiful cathedral right in the center of the city.

When I was there, it was a beautifully clean city. Of course, there were plenty of corner coffee shops which sold *gelato* (ice cream), cappuccino, and tasty pastries. To complement the picture-perfect post card there were some seven cinemas within a four-mile radius showing Indian, Italian, Arabic, and American movies. If one were to take photos of the city without its inhabitants, one would think Asmara to be like any other major metropolitan European city.

I had never really paid much attention to all the little incongruities associated with a "little Roma" plopped right on the edge of the Red Sea. I never had to because I didn't think that I would have to stay in this place. But now that I was stuck here, I started to look more closely at the inhabitants.

The people who lived in the city called themselves by their Italian name, *Asmarinos*, It's what they knew, and I know now not to fault them. But as a young girl, hearing all the Italian words and seeing the men wearing Italian sweaters and wool suits was a bit strange. I wondered how many of those beautifully dressed people with their fancy gold watches knew of the suffering of their brethren in the lowlands.

I became a recluse because everything seemed so unreal to me. I missed my village, my camels, my way of life so much that I withdrew. I was trying and failing to relate to this new urban environment. Though I was grateful to have my life and see my immediate family members safe, from my child's viewpoint, the city was dreadful. I felt completely disconnected with anyone I met in Asmara the entire time I was there.

I also didn't like what we did in Asmara. Back home, I lived a constant adventure. Here in the city, all we did was visit my mother's relatives. While I was grateful to every family member and friend for their support during this period, I often wondered, out loud, did we have to see each other every day? But, rather than try to maintain the energy required to endure a full afternoon of "chit chat," something I didn't understand at the time, I was much more content to remain at home. Claustrophobic, but quiet, I often chose our concrete walls over the invitations. So did my dad. I would see my mom when she came home to change clothes between social gatherings.

Sometimes, my mom tricked me into visiting by getting my cousins to cajole me into it. She knew what she was doing.

"You have to come," my cousin would insist. Usually it was Dahlia. She was close to my age, and we seemed to be able to understand each other on an adult level.

"Just get dressed and come with me."

"There's no emergency. I like being here. How about I show up at the next one?"

"Your mom won't let any of us eat until you get there. I'm not leaving without you." Off we went; I made the exception "this time."

At first, I found a way to rebel. I put on as brightly colored clothes as I could. They spoke to my core as nothing else did. They reminded me of my village, of its simplicity and peace, of the times when I was like a free little butterfly, flitting about as I pleased.

Chapter 2 • On Being a Refugee in My Own Country

"You can't wear those here," my mom finally told me, regarding those vivid garments. I complied. One more thing that used to bring me some happiness was now deemed out-of-place for the city.

I looked around at what the city women were wearing and began to learn that drab can also mean stylish. But while I had more clothes here in the city, like the shoes I was forced to wear, they were ugly. So, as usual, I decided to take matters into my own hands. A little of my creativity that used to express itself in our village all the time showed itself when I discovered an empty bucket.

In Tekreret, I guess you could say I pioneered a method for dying clothes, the Zebiba batik-in-a-bucket technique. Experimenting with my own clothes has always made me happy. The hand-dyed garments from our village were very saturated with dye and would often run when we washed them. In Tekreret, I exaggerated this and allowed the garments to bleed their colors up a line of buckets outside our hut. I tried to recreate this with a bucket I found in Asmara. I took a drab colored shirt and started its transformation. Unfortunately, my mom also chose this time to come home to change.

"What is this?" she demanded.

"Mom, I am just helping you. I'm cleaning."

"You are not. This water is redder than a tomato."

I didn't know what else to say, so I used the old, "I am just a kid, why are you picking on me?!" excuse.

My poor mom, she never has been able to understand my spirit, my need to express myself. Remember, that is not what a traditional Eritrean girl does. It has always baffled me a bit, actually. My mother has always been incredibly clever with her hands, weaving some amazingly beautiful baskets, but she was more concerned about keeping with tradition than allowing me—or her for that matter—to express her individuality. It didn't matter, however. Perhaps, it was because I wanted to drown out those killing-machine noises that I began to learn to listen to bright colors, a trick that no one else seemed to relate to. They simply made me happy, and they still do.

But, unfortunately, trying to create a little piece of happiness in the mess that the Ethiopian military were creating was impossible. In the end, most Eritreans did not have a choice; whether we lived in the lowlands or the cities, we all knew that we would eventually have to join the fighting or flee.

The ranks of the Freedom Fighters were growing—quickly. After years of ongoing raids, a large number of Eritreans finally decided that they wanted to see Eritrea as its own country—not merely a part of some other country—on a standard map. Around the same time, Ethiopia experienced a regime change that escalated the violence in Eritrea. Haile Selassie was deposed and eventually murdered by the Communist junta that overthrew him. Some sixty other high cabinet ministers were also killed. Unfortunately, the Communist regime of Ethiopia decided to follow the same line regarding the question of Eritrea, and equally unfortunate for Eritreans, the new rulers also had the backing of the Soviet Union and Cuba. They all came in full force to quash the Eritrean Freedom Fighters, which brought another level of confrontation between civilian Eritreans and the Ethiopian Communist Regime. Eritreans from all

Chapter 2 • On Being a Refugee in My Own Country

walks of life began to either flee the country for Sudan or enlist with the Eritrean Freedom Fighters.

To combat this new development, the Eritrean Freedom Fighters also began a campaign of influencing young Eritreans to join their fight to liberate Eritrea from the yolk of Ethiopia's occupation. Clandestine operations throughout Eritrean cities and towns were well underway. Even Eritreans who were part of the Eritrean diaspora, in places like Sudan and Saudi Arabia, were also recruited. Fortunately for Eritrean Independence, the recruitment efforts by Eritrean Freedom Fighters worked. Young Eritreans started joining the Eritrean Freedom Fighters in droves, and I wanted to be a part of the action.

By the time I was about fourteen years old, each village had a station where people would enlist to fight. I had lived in the city for about six years, and I had had enough. My friends and I formulated a plan whereby we would sneak out and join the Freedom Fighters. We had to do this in secret because no one's parents would ever permit this. It was dangerous, and death was a very real possibility.

I was excited about joining. I was strong, independent, and fearless. I also had an uncle who was a member of the *Fedain,* an elite corps of Freedom Fighters who would act as civilians, clandestinely living in a city or a village, under the occupying forces' nose. A *Fedain*'s job was to help deliver damaging blows to the important infrastructure and/or to the occupying forces themselves. For example, a *Fedain* would get orders to take out a particular person in the city who might have been a notorious occupiers' informer or an official whose death could cause the plummeting of morale to the military of the occupying forces.

I always admired my uncle. He looked like…well, he didn't look like a killer, but he had this look that said, "we will get our country back no matter what." Whenever he came to visit us, I would pretend to be asleep so that I could listen to him and my father talk about what was going on. I was fascinated and listened attentively. When my mother would come home, I would then pretend to wake up and "company" type conversation would ensue. But I think my uncle helped plant the seed for me to really want to become part of that special group who were fighting to gain Eritrean independence.

The day of reckoning finally arrived, and we put our plan into action. There were about six of us, boys and girls, and we knew that everything depended upon our traveling significantly far from Asmara; we planned on walking for two days. This way, we figured, none of our parents would be able to trace us. We had to pick a day when everyone was busy doing their normal routines. My dad spent his days at a job he found once we had arrived in the city; my little brother, Yasin, was in school; and my mother was away on one of her endless visits to the relatives.

On this very important day, I told my mother I wasn't feeling well as she was leaving to visit with my cousins. She knew me well enough to know that it took a lot for me to say I was not feeling well. It really worked because she totally believed me. She didn't question it. "Just rest," she said. "I am going to visit some of your cousins."

I thought to myself "Yeah, you're always visiting someone—." As much as I was happy that my mother believed my story, I was resentful at the same time because the least I felt she could have done was stay with me and take care

Chapter 2 • On Being a Refugee in My Own Country

of me for a day that I was "not feeling well." But, as usual, my mother had important things to tend to. Perhaps my resentment had to do with a little part of me that was afraid; I didn't know what was going to happen.

But I quickly placed all those feelings aside, for I was too eager to leave the city with my friends and join the struggle than to give any lasting thought to what irked me about my mother. As soon as she left, I dressed, grabbed a few things I thought I would need, and met my friends. The borders of the city were heavily patrolled by Ethiopian soldiers; it was not easy to escape. We accomplished this by dressing like kids from the country and saying we were off to gather wood for fuel from the surrounding countryside.

I was prepared to walk all day, but after two hours everyone else was ready to quit and return home. "How are any of you going to be Freedom Fighters? You can't even walk!" I growled.

"Don't you get tired?" they whimpered.

"How are we going to fight the Ethiopian soldiers if we are going to rest every couple hours?" I shot back.

The city kids wimped out. They demanded that we stop at the next recruit station. I was irritated, but I gave in. We walked for a total of six hours and stopped at the very first village we arrived at that had a recruiting office. I didn't like it. I knew that it wouldn't take long for my mom to find me there. I knew my mom would go to the first and second villages with recruiting offices and would keep looking until she found me.

So at the first office that we found, we began the process of registration. I reasoned that I best sign up at that point; I knew traveling alone was out of the question. The Freedom

Fighter in command informed us that training started on the same day of enlisting. Even though I stayed with my "comrades," I had a feeling that we shouldn't have stopped so soon.

I admired the Eritrean Freedom Fighters for many reasons. I was especially fascinated by how fast they ate their food. Imagine the coarsest grain that you could have and then add lentils to it; that is basically what they ate. We were given the same basic rations. Though more substantial than white bread, we were not accustomed to it. I thought the food was just fine. It was definitely more nutritious than the white bread that I had been eating in the city. When one of my friends, a city girl, vomited, I immediately thought, "This girl needs to go back. She's not going to make it. She's not going to survive."

First we were interviewed as a group. The Eritrean fighter interviewing us looked tough, and rightfully so. I could tell that they had been fighting this war for a long time, and that he had lost many of his fellow Freedom Fighters.

I was also very familiar with the Freedom Fighter demeanor because they had been in and out of my village ever since I could remember. Even when I was little, I would ask my uncle a lot of questions. My mom said it was strange for a child to be so interested in these matters, but I was fascinated. Because of my uncle, I had adult knowledge the other kids lacked.

The recruiter immediately started asking us pointed questions. He wanted to find out what kind of fighters we would make. When it came to be my turn, I answered his questions directly. He was demanding, which I didn't like,

Chapter 2 • On Being a Refugee in My Own Country

but I thought, "well if that's how they get the job done, then so be it."

But everything changed when he asked me, "will you do whatever you are ordered to do?"

I looked him square in the eye and answered, "I will not kill women and children."

The recruiter couldn't believe what he was hearing. He said, "You will do exactly as you are ordered to do."

I don't remember what I said or was about to say because at that point, I heard my mother's voice. She was arguing with one of the Freedom Fighters. He was insisting that I should be able to join. My mother was demanding that I be let go, and somehow, it came out who my uncle was.

As I left the recruiting office, the officer who interviewed me said, "Why didn't you tell me who your uncle was?"

I just glared at him.

His parting shot to me was, "You should join the Peace Corps."

I was crying hysterically as we left the office. I had set my heart on joining the Freedom Fighters and helping my country win its independence from Ethiopia. I was throwing a tantrum because I wasn't allowed to do so. But my hysterics were nothing compared to the state my mother was in. She was inconsolable. Her two sons were already out of the country—her oldest in America and the second in Saudi Arabia. Most of her friend's children had joined the Freedom Fighters and some had been killed.

Fortunately, she was able to hear what I told her next: "Mom, look, I can't live in Eritrea. Either you send me out of here, or I'll try to join again. And next time, I will go far, far away and you won't find me." She knew she would have to let me go.

As I left the station, I thought about what the recruiting officer said to me. Why should I "join the Peace Corps" when my country needed me? I was extremely upset and felt like both my mother and this recruiting officer were thwarting my great desire to help.

But, in a flash, it all came together for me where my life was going to be headed. I would still be able to help my fellow Eritreans, even if I fled. I just didn't know how yet.

CHAPTER 3

Fleeing Towards Freedom: Out of Eritrea and into the Sudan

It wasn't long after my mother found me at the Freedom Fighter outpost that my favorite aunt, my mother's sister, Ne'rit, came to Eritrea from the Sudan. She had long since fled our country and had been living in the Sudan for years, but had to make the very dangerous journey back to Eritrea to get her son and his family out. I was very happy to see her.

At this point, the Ethiopian soldiers were becoming more and more brutal toward the people in the cities. The Ethiopian military had also completely disconnected Eritrea from the rest of the world. And it was very degrading, the way the Ethiopian soldiers treated us, whether we stayed in Eritrea or were attempting to escape.

There was one street in Asmara, for example, that the Ethiopian soldiers had declared off limits to the Eritreans. It was known as the Rodeo Drive of Asmara, and the Ethiopian military had decided that it was "too good" for Eritreans. The soldiers also kept Eritreans away from the areas where the Ethiopians lived or any important governmental head resided. This is actually very typical of any colonizing country to treat the colonized people in this way. The colonizer will go to great lengths to demoralize and oppress the colonized.

Not only was the oppression becoming increasingly difficult to bear, it was also becoming more dangerous. The Ethiopians were notorious for making civilian Eritreans "disappear." Or the Ethiopian soldiers would take civilians, kill them, and leave them in the street. Mothers wanted their children to flee the country. I couldn't agree with them more. I felt extremely unsafe in Asmara—just like when my family and I left Tekreret.

Perhaps worst of all, however, was the Ethiopian soldiers had started bombing indiscriminately. Even though the soldiers said their mission was to eliminate the Freedom Fighters and not the Eritrean people, they were lying. The Ethiopians weren't just bombing Freedom Fighter enclaves; their bombs were falling all over Eritrea—in the cities and on the villages—and it was really just thinly disguised ethnic cleansing.

When the Ethiopian Communist military junta took over Haile Selassie's government, what they did made the brutality meted out by the former dictator pale in comparison. The Ethiopian communists were cold and merciless. In fact, Ethiopia's Communist leader, Mengistu, made it chillingly clear that Ethiopia did not need Eritreans; it only needed their land. Therefore, bombing anything and everything was just part of that genocidal mind-set.

So when my Aunt Ne'rit came back to Asmara to take more of her family out, I saw this as my chance to escape the hell that was all around me. Asmara was never "home"

Chapter 3 • Fleeing Towards Freedom

to me, and there was no Tekreret left at that point, so the decision was fairly easy. I told my Aunt that I wanted to go back with her.

Aunt Ne'rit really was like a second mother to me, and I loved her deeply. She had married a man from the lowlands, lived in a nearby village, and introduced my mother to my father. I also thought that she was more motherly than my own. Aunt Ne'rit spent a lot of time with her children, and I always liked how she treated them. She was less inclined to visit relatives and friends just for the sake of visiting. During the week that she spent in Asmara, I spent a lot more time with her than with my mom. I knew that going with her, I would be well cared for. So along with her son and his family, we all fled Asmara together.

Fleeing was not an easy task. It really had a dynamic all its own because we weren't safe on either side. The Ethiopian soldiers under the new communist regime still considered everyone a Freedom Fighter, and the Freedom Fighters continually needed all the able bodies it could get because, after all, they were fighting the most powerful army in Africa at the time—the Ethiopian military—and the troops needed to be constantly replenished.

So in the middle of that melee, I left my mother, father, and younger brother behind in Asmara. I wondered if I would ever see them again, if I would be captured and murdered by the Ethiopian soldiers like so many young Eritreans who had tried to flee before me. But I had to go. So with Aunt Ne'rit, we crossed the border into Sudan.

She had already arranged for a camel man/smuggler to carry our food and belongings. In order to get to Sudan, every Eritrean had to escape during the night because the

Building the Impossible: A Refugee's Journey of Giving Back

Ethiopian military would bomb us during the day. And we had to walk. No-one could fly out of Eritrea. While the airport in Asmara was still functional, the Ethiopian government did not allow planes of any kind to take Eritreans out of the country. Needless to say, because of the bombings, traveling through Eritrea was perhaps more dangerous at that point than when we fled our village the first time.

Over half a million Eritreans sought refuge in Sudan during the thirty-year war with the Ethiopian military. The Sudan borders Eritrea to the north, and we had to travel through miles and miles of hostile territory, most of Eritrea actually, to get to the safety of the Sudanese border. We hid in many places on the way to survive the bombings. We carried the minimum amount of belongings, not much more than the clothes on our back. The majority of our traveling was conducted in the company of the stars. the moon shining bright, and the sense of serene quietness engulfing us. The only noise one could hear was the gentle steps of the camel, some frogs whistling in their odd way, and other creatures that I could not decipher from the wilderness beyond. I remember thinking how loud silence really is and how strong a presence it has, as the camels made their slow, steady progress through the desert.

During the day, the camel man would hide us in small villages along the way. It was actually wonderful to be that close to a camel again, if even for a short while. Also, I was totally confident in our smuggler. We relied upon him to take us to prearranged locations where we knew we'd be safe until night fell again, and we could be on our way. A portion of what my aunt had paid him must have taken care of this.

Chapter 3 • Fleeing Towards Freedom

It was very dark when we traveled, but in spite of the dangers, I was glad to just be out of the city. Part of our escape route took us through the area of Tekreret, or what was left of it anyway. Aunt Ne'rit was paying close attention to my moves at this point. She actually never took her eyes off me, during those dangerous times when my childhood curiosity could have easily gotten me killed. She knew that, because this was familiar territory to me, I would venture out by myself as soon as I could. I'm sure I actually wandered off many times into different areas that could have proven lethal.

I actually have always had a tendency to venture into the wilderness. I love the feeling of being alone in the jungle; it has always given me a wonderful sense of peace because there, I feel totally free. It allows me to make my space huge. It was actually a relief to my spirit to be back in the jungle after all the concrete and confined little boxes of Asmara.

So one night, I wandered off. I needed some space, and I think part of it, too, was that I just wanted to go in a different direction. We were so confined as we traveled and were kept on a tight schedule with very tight restrictions.

As I ventured off into the wee hours of the night, I relied on my sense of smell, perhaps, and the stars and the moon beyond the horizon to find my way. I found that the city hadn't taken away my ability to navigate through the date palm and banana trees.

It wasn't long until I returned to the caravan safe and sound, but everyone was frightened. To say it was very dangerous to travel in the jungle alone doesn't quite capture how incredibly perilous it really was. I had taken my life into my own hands when I went on my little jaunt. Even the camel man started following me around after that.

It took us between a week and half and two weeks to travel from Asmara to the safety of Sudan. My recollection of this ghostly caravan mostly rests in its eerily calming effect. For miles and miles, it was a cadence—our breathing accompanied by the heavier swoosh of the camel's breath, and always the very soft glide of the camel's padded feet on the sand. Because there was so much stuff loaded on the camels for our journey, we had to take turns riding on a camel's back. I didn't mind walking though. My aunt also did her best to keep us on track and moving forward while at the same time keeping us all calm. In the manner typical to Eritreans, she accomplished all this without ever mentioning any of it.

We never encountered any Ethiopian soldiers during our flight through Eritrea, but Eritrean Freedom Fighters did stop us for questioning at one check point. This particular group of fighters had moved through a village to eat. It was the same village we were staying in for that particular day. When they questioned us, my aunt assured them we lived in that specific location. Fortunately, we were dressed similarly to the others in that village because she had already traveled this escape route. She knew what to expect along the way, but it was still very tense—definitely a close call.

Fortunately, our journey was uneventful after that. We made it to the Sudan, and this is the first time I encountered the refugee camps. Because I lived with my Aunt, I wasn't required to live in them. And that, fortunately, allowed me the opportunity to fall in love with my northern neighbors.

Chapter 3 • Fleeing Towards Freedom

The Sudanese are amazing people; without hesitation, they welcomed Eritrean and Ethiopian refugees alike as we fled in droves from our homeland. I loved it there. The people are beautiful. They are kind and generous; they have great souls and are not judgmental.

Also, when I was there, the Sudan and its people were so peaceful. The kindness and generosity of the adult Sudanese I felt came from a very innocent place inside of them.

To hear that the Sudanese have adopted the war-like attitudes of many other African countries leaves me not only dumbfounded but chagrined. It makes me feel especially sad now to see the Sudan in a continual crisis of civil war. Other African countries seem to have no problem with civil war or attacking a neighboring country. However, the people I met while I was in the Sudan were not warriors. They savored a way of living that was so kind, and they were quick to share this with everyone who entered their country.

This was nowhere more apparent than with their traditions surrounding food—traditions I know continue today. I had always been thin. This was compounded by the fact I loved walking. But when I got to the Sudan and experienced their delicious food, I just ate and ate. The quality of the food is always fresh and they never prepare just one dish of any particular thing. Okra could be offered in three or four variations at one time. Sautéed vegetables are cooked with very tender lamb or goat, all fresh from that day. They prepare grains like rice with a rich combination of spices. Their first break for food usually happens around 10 a.m. This is called *fotour*. Everything stops in both villages and cities, and if the Sudanese see you walking by, you are immediately asked to join in the feast.

Eritreans have many endearing stories and legends of the Sudanese. One of my favorites deals with the colonization and extensive occupation by England. After World War II, when it became time for the British to hand back the country through a signed agreement, the Sudanese were preparing for their daily *fotour*. The British were ready with the treaty and wanted the Sudanese to sign. The Sudanese said, "Join us for *fotour*, then we'll sign!" They seemed to have learned the secret of how much more amicable people are to each other when they share their food.

But as civil war took over that wonderful country, many of the Eritreans left. No one knows how many Eritreans, generations of refugees at this point, currently live in the Sudan. As of 2015, the UN Refugee Agency UNHCR, reports that the official number of Eritrean refugees in Sudan is around 92,000. But this report also notes that there are many more who haven't been counted because these are people who consider themselves permanent residents and only refugees and "asylum seekers," are counted.[1]

Economic issues have always been a factor for Eritreans living in Sudan and other neighboring countries. During my short sojourn there, many of the Eritrean refugees left the Sudan, because it simply didn't have as much opportunity as the very rich country that sits across the Red Sea that is bursting, literally, with oil. In the early 1970s, Saudi Arabia's economy was booming beyond comprehension. The "petro-dollar" was abundant and Saudi Arabia was

---

[1] Ahmed Saeed. "Sudan's Eritrean refugees flee for 'money and freedom': Refugees' accounts cite grinding economic conditions and repression among reason for fleeing Eritrea. 2 July, 2015. http://www.aljazeera.com/news/2015/06/sudan-eritrean-refugees-flee-money-freedom-150629114157143.html. Accessed 6 December, 2016

Chapter 3 • Fleeing Towards Freedom

developing at a break-neck speed. Even the Sudanese were traveling to Saudi Arabia for work.

I knew I would not be happy in either place. As I had walked those two fraught weeks through the Eritrean lowlands and into the Sudan, I had formed a plan. My feet plodding on the African sand marched to the same phrase that kept me alive during the Ethiopian soldiers' raids on my village, "there must be something better than this… there must be something better than this…."

The cadence of that phrase became a promise. My village was bombed beyond recognition. My homeland was being propelled on a trajectory I knew I could neither help nor control. The fabled land of America, the "land of the free" beckoned, and in my heart of hearts, I understood that is where I would finally land.

I stayed with Aunt Ne'rit for about a year, but as the inevitable day of departure from the Sudan approached, I started to imaginatively shape my journey to America as a series of train stations. Saudi Arabia was simply the next stop.

CHAPTER 4

Finally My First Taste of Freedom

I was no different than the vast majority of Eritrean refugees. Many of us sought refuge in Saudi Arabia at some point in our journey. While many Eritreans have chosen to make that their permanent home, I knew from the moment I arrived, I wouldn't stay long.

Eritreans are a hard-working people, and we gave the Saudis a large labor force to take care of the more menial jobs. I think, too, that the Saudis respected our intention to help those who had remained in Eritrea. It was, in fact, an unspoken but hard-and-fast rule that if you were working in Saudi Arabia, you were to send money and clothes back home.

The Saudis were also a little in awe of what we had to endure at the hands of the Ethiopian soldiers and our continual willingness to stand up and fight.

Most Eritreans, including myself, had to support ourselves with menial jobs. We were the housekeepers and the Eritrean men were the chauffeurs, if we were lucky. I was hired to be the nanny for three Saudi children, aged three to nine, and my responsibilities also included domestic chores. But while I was essentially their housekeeper, this Saudi couple honored me with their respect. This set the tone for their kids. This was my first official occupation that involved working with children.

In the late 1970s and early 1980s, the Saudi oil economy had created a whole infrastructure of business and industry that generated incredible wealth. Many Saudis lived an opulent, affluent life, based on this oil economy. The family I worked for lived a more middle-class existence. The father was not a Saudi businessman; he was a professor of English Literature at the University of Riyadh.

Part of what made me want to leave Saudi Arabia was that women were too strictly confined. Freedom and independence were not something that we had much of there. What cemented my decision to leave, however, was an event I still think about. It highlighted how little control I had over my body and the decisions being made about it, and looking back, I'm always a little shocked at my audacity.

In most countries of the Middle East, Africa and Asia, men feel that any woman's body part belongs to them. It is typical for a woman to be pinched or grabbed in public, and I was no exception. One particular afternoon my close friend, Muna, and I were enjoying the beautiful outdoor market, located in the old part of Riyadh. One man in particular followed us for quite some time, pinching and grabbing both of us at different intervals. At that time, we were around fifteen to seventeen years old. We knew we couldn't complain nor say anything directly to this man, and he knew it too.

He was relentless. We decided that it was best to just give up our precious afternoon out and return home. We were

Chapter 4 • Finally My First Taste of Freedom

mad because we were only allowed out of the house to go walking, and going to the market was our only source of entertainment. So this awful man had cut short our only respite from the boredom we so often faced during the day.

But this man was different than most. Even without the camouflage of the crowded market, this pervert kept right on following us, pinching and grabbing. He was expressionless, but his actions told us that he perversely enjoyed the power he had over our lives at that particular moment. We had been taught to just look straight ahead, to not talk back, and to keep moving forward when faced with such circumstances. We also knew that the police wouldn't help us if we called for them. The police typically sided with the male adults, so confronting him or creating a scene would just work against us in some distorted fashion.

He followed us all the way to where we were living. This beastly man was pushing his luck without realizing it. When we got to the door, with the man still pinching and grabbing, Muna and I walked into the house. But instead of just continuing to walk behind Muna, I did something very brash. I turned and confronted him. I had had enough. Typical to all Middle Eastern homes, sandals are left outside the front door. As he advanced towards me again, his expressionless face connected with the full, flat surface of the sandal that had found its way into my hand. Behind me, Muna froze. The impact was strong; it had in it all of the anger I had bottled up in me as this idiot had been pestering and harassing us, as well as the frustration that I had with my situation in Saudi Arabia in general.

After I hit him, the sandal flew out of my hand. My eyes locked with his. He knew from my expression that he'd better not try anything else. He surprised both Muna and me by snatching the fallen sandal and then disappearing down the narrow street, running all the way without a backward glance. I felt fantastically relieved, but upset and very worried about the sandal that disappeared.

I left shortly thereafter for Italy.

• • •

Despite the contrary opinions of everyone around me, I never doubted for a second that I would be traveling to Italy from Saudi Arabia. Italy was the destination of my heart. It also happened to be the way that most Eritrean refugees made it to the United States at that time. When you are travelling as a refugee, you never take anything for granted, but I just knew I would get to Italy.

The Catholic Community Services, based in Rome, made it possible for many Africans to get to America by sponsoring us, and I must commend them for their humanitarian efforts. This service has helped many Eritreans and other East Africans to settle throughout the United States without any expectations in return. They were simply doing their religious duty to help human beings who had fled oppressive and violent regimes. They were doing God's work, and religious beliefs or race didn't matter.

Any act of colonization is fraught with prejudice and oppression. While Italy was certainly kinder and more helpful to the Eritreans than other colonizers—the Turks in the Ottoman Empire or the English after World War II—the Italians still colonized us. Colonizers do certain things to try to camouflage the social and political suppression

Chapter 4 • Finally My First Taste of Freedom

they inflict on their subjects. On one hand, there was a "hand-shake," but on the other there was a "slap," and the line between the two were always so blurred that they were almost simultaneous in their delivery.

The Italian hand-shake came in the form of building infrastructures that Eritreans enjoyed. But the slap hurt because these state-of-the-art roads were built with the natives' indentured labor. The Italians improved the terrain and the plateaus of the highland, built highways between Asmara and Massawa—the all-important Red Sea port— and improved the train system there and in other parts of the country, but again, on the backs of native labor paid subsistence wages. Eritreans were only allowed a fourth-grade level of education under Italian rule, and the postcard picture of Asmara being the little Roma, with its boulevards and gelato parlors, were meant for the pleasure of the colonizers, not Eritreans.

But ambiguity lives on both sides, and the Italians did much to help Eritrea develop and modernize. The British—the empire that took control from Italy—did nothing of the sort.

The destruction began after the close of World War II. As part of the various treaties that ended that war, the Italians were forced to give up Eritrea to England in 1941. Eritrea was placed under British colonial rule initially with a military administration until the Allied forces could determine its fate. The first thing the British did was remove the Eritrean industries in Asmara and Massawa—industries the Italians created—to other African countries colonized by England.

Although the British liberalized Eritrean education by allowing Eritreans to become as educated as they wanted, the damage that the English did was insurmountable. While they occupied Eritrea for only ten years, I truly believed they were the worst colonizers. They pillaged the resources and degraded the people. Perhaps we were feeling the brunt of English anger. During their occupation of Eritrea, they were in the throes of giving India back to its people. Because of this beleaguered history of my homeland, I have long admired Mahatma Gandhi and his dogged insistence that his people be free of English colonial rule.

The English governed Eritrea until 1952. During that time, there was much wrangling in the U.N. over what to do with the country. The western powers were concerned that Eritrea, left to its own devices, would become either Arab dominated or communist ruled, neither of which would have been advantageous for the West. This is why the U.N. decided that Eritrea would be "federated" by Ethiopia.

Of course, as I have noted previously, Selassie wanted the Eritrean coast, and the English basically handed it to him on a silver tea platter. The English bowed to his more powerful military. Not only did Selassie immediately start the village raids, he completely disabled all that the Italians had built. Anything that the Italians had modernized, Selassie took back to Ethiopia. Furthermore, Selassie took up with gusto the British ability to divide and conquer. He actively created strife between the different ethnic and religious groups in Eritrea which helped further his colonization campaign.

Politics aside, however, most of my friends and family in Saudi Arabia never believed I'd really leave for Italy. It was actually expected that I would stay in Saudi Arabia,

Chapter 4 • Finally My First Taste of Freedom

marry, have my five kids, and send money home for the rest of my life. My mother especially wanted me to stay. She had grown quite accustomed to me sending her money, gold, and clothes. My dad was more willing to accept that I was off to Italy. He knew me well and had raised me to be independent enough to know that if I wanted to go to Italy, there was nothing that was going to stop me from doing so.

I was probably eighteen or nineteen years old at this point and had spent the majority of my teenage years in a country whose law forbids women to do much of anything. For me, the idea of Italy was magical. It was *Roma.*

I can't really describe the relief I felt in Italy. After all those years of escaping the Ethiopian soldiers and dealing with the Saudi laws, I finally felt safe. When I stepped foot in Rome, I experienced my first taste of real freedom since leaving my village. It was the first time since I fled Tekreret that I felt that I could breathe again. I didn't have to watch what I said or did; I could wear what I wanted, and even eat and drink what I wanted. I had choices for the first time in a long time, and I relished that immensely. I would go dancing with fellow Eritreans, and I loved it. I would dance by myself or with others, it didn't matter. It was the first time since I had raced camels so many years prior that I felt like my body was mine to control.

I started taking longer and longer walks by myself, and it really was heavenly, surrounded by that wonderful and compelling Eternal City. The rush of independence that I felt every time I walked out of my door never grew old.

There really is nothing like the feeling of freedom after being confined by custom or practically paralyzed by fear. I could exist in a way in wherein I did not have to worry about anybody stopping me for no reason or restricting me on where I could go.

But I knew that I wouldn't stay long in Italy, no matter how enchanted I was. My oldest brother, Saleh, was already in the United States with his family. He had procured my passage to America, and I was scheduled to travel to Minnesota where his family lived. They were waiting for Saleh to find a house in California so they could move there with him.

I don't think Minnesota was his first choice of places to settle in the U.S.; it certainly wasn't mine. But because Saleh had arrived in St. Paul, Minnesota in 1973 to attend university and become a Nurse Anesthetist, that's where his family—his wife and children and then me—would have to land first before we could move to a warmer climate.

CHAPTER 5

America! At Last

So that's how it happened. After those many long years of fleeing for my life and not feeling settled anywhere, I was finally in America.

I was beyond excited. I had *made* it. But I immediately experienced a shock. My unceremonious touch down happened at the St. Paul, Minnesota airport in the middle of winter. It was freezing. I had never been so cold in my entire life.

On the way home from the airport, I couldn't believe my eyes. It was drab and overcast, a typical winter day in Minnesota, and there was snow everywhere, deep piles of it. This was definitely not my idea of what America should look like. So from my first minutes on the ground in Minnesota, I knew that I wanted to be in California ASAP, and no one would be able to convince me otherwise. But I didn't say anything about that yet. I thought it would be rude.

My driver seemed not to notice the cold. He talked proudly about the thousand lakes that existed throughout St. Paul. He told me we were driving right over one of them and this was possible because it was frozen.

"Okay, you're telling me that we're driving over a lake?!" I said. That was almost too much. It was comforting to know that Saleh was in California as well as a few friends. I couldn't wait to see them.

So my first morning in America found me staring out into this foreign world of cold, wet cotton. I was intimidated for about five minutes, then put on every bit of clothing I could find and went out into the white landscape. I was finally here, and I was going to find out what this city was all about.

When the white stuff was falling from the sky, I noticed that it wasn't that cold after all. The last thing I took with me before I left the house was an umbrella. It worked for rain, why not snow?

I have since noticed something that is particular to Americans; people are comfortable speaking to you, all the time. In Europe and in Asia, people tend to keep to themselves. Not in Minnesota, and not generally in America. Everyone has something to say, and while I can't tell you what these people were actually saying to me on that first cold morning in Minnesota, they were all very friendly about it.

I have found over the years that the American willing- ness to chat opens up a healing connection that I've not found in other parts of the world. That was amazing to me when I first got to America, and I still think it's lovely that people are willing to say "Hi! How are you," to a complete stranger. I was also amazed at how my new compatriots dressed. They were wearing huge, bulky clothing, and their faces were red and pink. I had never seen anything like it
in my entire life.

My first thought was that they were so strange. Why were they all speaking to me? Instantly I began to wonder, "Do I look that different? Can they tell I just arrived? That I am

Chapter 5 • America! At Last

from across the Atlantic, half a world away?" I soon realized that they weren't staring at me, just at the umbrella I had opened over my head during a light, Minnesota snowfall. It seemed that an umbrella wasn't the proper accessory after all, even though it still makes infinite sense to me to use one when it snows!

Ten minutes into my first walk, I was freezing and went right back home. I called Saleh, reaching him at his apartment in Freemont, CA. "I am moving to California," was all I said and hung up. My brother Saleh had a very powerful presence and was used to being in command. Fortunately, even though he didn't know me well at the time, he sensed when not to fight me. He agreed to bring me to California as soon as he could. I lasted in St. Paul for a few months.

I decided that before I went to California, I should lose some weight. I had always been thin, but my sedentary lifestyle in Sudan and Saudi—and the excellent food that I ate and ate in Sudan— had made me chunky. One of the more modern girls from our circle of Eritrean friends told me that smoking was the best and fastest way to lose weight. I didn't even like the smell of cigarettes, but I was determined to slim down. I thought if I held my breath that this would help me smoke more effectively and thus lose weight more quickly.

Saleh was mortified. As a Nurse Anesthetist, he immediately began to list everything that would happen to me if I kept on smoking. I'd burn my lungs; I'd get cancer; I would die, or at the very least, I'd get sick. I only smoked for three days. I really couldn't stand the smell and how it made me feel. Ironically, Saleh smoked. He did have a better way for me to lose weight, but that had to wait for our time in California.

One of the few things that really kept me sane during that long cold winter in Minnesota was that Saleh's house had a huge basement. It seemed larger than the house above. I cleaned that bottom area beyond anyone's expectations, and the basement became the only place where I could express some of the new freedom I had just experienced in Rome.

It was my private universe of music and dance, and it was a great way to release my teenage anxieties. I would dance down there every day, sometimes for hours, with my eyes shut. I loved the fact that I could just simply start dancing. I would dance with my eyes open, leaping around and on top of the furniture. Dancing has always been a way for me to feel alive, free, and liberated from all inhibitions. I didn't need to go looking for my shawl or worry about what the religious police in Saudi Arabia would think. So during my first months in America, in that basement in Minnesota, I danced and danced and finally felt free.

CHAPTER 6

California, Here I Come!

I don't remember the trip from Minnesota to California. I never really remember the actual travel of my journeys. Leaving is always hard for me, I suspect, because of how I had to leave Tekreret.

What I wasn't at all sad about, however, was leaving the Minnesota winter behind. I had never been so cold in my life. I literally didn't have the blood for that northern climate, having lived most of my life in the part of the world where there was one temperature—hot. I had a friend in San Francisco and one in L.A., and all they could do was talk about the weather and how beautiful California was. I was thrilled to find myself in the land of my dreams.

On my very first morning in California, Saleh woke me up at the crack of dawn with a brown polyester jogging suit in his hand. It was the same brown as my shoes in Asmara, and I had no idea what jogging was, but the weather was nice, and I was up for an adventure.

I got up, went to the window, looked out on my newfound heaven, and decided that this was going to be a marvelous day. I zipped into my suit, ready for anything, and we drove to Lake Elizabeth and started jogging. I fell instantly in love, both with California and jogging.

California delivered everything that was promised, and jogging, well, jogging was like breathing. Feeling my body move freely, breathing rhythmically, sensing the rush of fresh air in my face, I knew that I had found, finally, something that could give me what I had lost all those years ago when I had to abandon my palm trees and warm, alive air in Eritrea. I had found a place that I could call home.

Saleh hardly knew me when we lived in Eritrea, since he grew up away from our mother. Traveling away from the home of my birth completed my family, in a way. Once I was in the States, Saleh served as a father figure. We were staying in a small apartment in Northern California while Saleh searched for a house. Jogging around the lake became our family time. Not only was I beginning to shed all of my traveling fat, I was developing a good relationship with my older brother.

I'm always a little amazed, thinking about our strong personalities, that we were able to share that one-bedroom apartment so peacefully. I think because jogging every day around Lake Elizabeth served as the basis of our communication, we were able to get to know each other better. It was a very special time for me because we were able to share with each other how we viewed this new world we were becoming a part of. I even learned to listen to Saleh's advice when it felt right to me, but I could challenge him and have my own opinions on any subject.

In America, I had a voice, and coming from a part of the world where women do not often have a voice, this was empowering. I also just simply enjoyed the freedom of being able to have some simple, fun competition with my brother. I would always challenge him when we jogged.

Chapter 6 • California, Here I Come!

"How many times did you go around the lake?" I'd ask him. He'd roll his eyes and then pick a number of times that was less than mine.

Saleh worked all day in the hospital, sometimes even a double shift, and then he played soccer with his friends. He was tired, but he always played along with me. I loved everything about my new passion. I think Saleh began to regret what he had introduced me to.

One day when I was pestering Saleh, again about jogging, he asked, somewhat in exasperation, "Well, do you have any other hobbies that you like?.

"Dancing is fun. I like to go to clubs," I said.

"Impossible," he said. "You are under age, and that's not happening in California."

Without realizing it, my curiosity regarding a separate issue presented a solution to this problem. I told him, "I want to see where black Americans live. I see them all the time on TV shows, living in cities. Where are they?"

I wondered just how much energy Saleh actually consumed, for he seemed to always stay one step ahead of me in those days.

"Okay, one Sunday I'll take you," he said, referring to the area where black Americans lived.

It didn't take long for that Sunday to come. We got in the car and started driving.

Saleh, as I mentioned before, is a strong person, and he recognized that I am not a follower. He liked that I constantly challenged him. He was also a highly opinionated and outspoken person, far more suited for politics than for medicine. But he saw the importance of showing me all there was to this United States of America.

So on this particular Sunday, we drove to Oakland, which is about thirty minutes from where we lived. Most of the businesses we drove past were closed, but there seemed to be an endless offering of fast food restaurants. Those were all open, along with many churches and liquor stores.

Then, before I saw anything else, I heard the music. One building we were driving past was exploding with energy and sound; really soulful music. People were dressed very elegantly and in joyous colors. I saw hats moving with feathers.

Unbeknownst to me, I had discovered my first Oakland Gospel church. Because it was Sunday, people were pouring in for service. I wanted to see what it was all about. We weren't dressed well enough, but I wasn't going to let that stop us. I insisted we go in. We were both laughing as we entered and were swept up into the spirit of that blessed place.

The rest of that day belonged to my brother's plans. We drove from Oakland to San Francisco. He showed me neighborhoods of every race and economic level. He explained the different ethnic areas as we drove through them. Saleh also talked about their languages, traditions, and customs. It was the first-hand kind of education that I liked the most, and I learned much. Our field trip concluded with a visit to Golden Gate Park. Of course, it was the perfect place to jog, and I got back to the Park via the Bay Area transit system the very next day.

For the following months, at least once a week, you could find me running along the paths in that beautiful park. When I was done running, I explored. San Francisco reminded me a little bit of Italy; a person could just walk and walk. I walked up and down those amazing hills and

Chapter 6 • California, Here I Come!

saw fantastic things. It was the best exercise anyone could ever get.

While Saleh was getting a reprieve from jogging with me, he was still trying to find an alternative way of exercising closer to home that would interest me, preferably one that didn't include him. He tried taking me to health clubs. I was intrigued by the health club-craze that was happening in the eighties, but the only way Saleh would take me inside was if I promised not to say anything until we were back outside. I couldn't believe the first step class I witnessed. People standing in one place, tapping their feet on a slab of plastic and concentrating as though nothing else existed seemed very strange to me. It seemed like, for these people, exercise was work, not pleasurable or fun.

Life was interesting. During the time we lived together, I watched Saleh read an entire book in two or three days. He was voracious. He instilled in me the love of reading. All of the books he brought me bridged the gap between my being able to just read English to actually speaking it. But the way I learned how to really speak the language was through music.

I love music, and not just because it inspires me to dance. Listening to American music helped me learn how to actively speak English, and during my early days in America, I had to make a choice between being entertained by music and using music to learn English. I loved to dance to R & B and its offshoot, Funk. But Country Music was my music of choice for listening because its pace is slower, and I could understand the lyrics, which helped me with my English even more. I think also that for a young woman who had been deprived of so much sensory experience during her teenaged years, country songs also touched a romantic nerve in me. They contained every day commentary as well as deep observations about how men and women relate to each other, or at least attempt to. Barbara Mandrell, Dolly Parton, Randy Travis—I love them and still listen to country music.

I stayed with Saleh in California for about a year until his wife and family moved from Minnesota. He had bought a beautiful house, and while I was welcome to stay, I felt that it was important that I make it on my own. I discovered something that is still amazing to me—Job Core.

For Americans, Job Core is the place of last resort for the kids that didn't make it in regular high school. For me, a kid who had grown up in a war zone with no regular school, let alone primary, secondary, or high school education, this was a Godsend. It was like boarding school! Because English was my second language, I was taking English classes. I was also preparing for my GED while doing vocational classes. I picked banking as the profession I wanted to learn. I liked the work, but I had to dress in business clothes every day, including nylons. I hated them. I didn't last long in banking.

Job Core also gave me something even more important, something that really can only happen in America—an independence that I never experienced anywhere else. It also gave me discipline. I had to learn how to live life as a responsible adult. We lived in dorms, and so we had to get up, make our beds straight, and make sure our rooms were clean (in fact the supervisors checked our rooms every day).

I couldn't help but long every once in a while for my bed roll in Tekreret. But I took pride in keeping my little room clean. Once I got written up because I had two roommates

Chapter 6 • California, Here I Come!

and our room wasn't as clean as it was supposed to be. I protested—how could I ever get written up for not being clean? My councilor tried to reassure me that everyone got written up a few times; it was no big deal. But I was indignant and vowed never to have that happen again. After that, I would check after my roommates left to make sure everything was exactly the way it was supposed to be.

Living with Saleh and then participating in Job Core gave me wonderful, important life lessons. I will always be grateful for these opportunities, and for both my big brother and my Job Core counselor who encouraged and challenged me to excel.

As my English improved, Saleh also continued to mentor me. He wanted me to explore what was possible in America. He told me, "read as much as you can, find out what you really love, don't worry how much time you spend on a subject or even a major in school. If you find out that it isn't something you're interested in, if it's not your love and passion, then leave it alone."

I took his advice and for the next two years; I did what I call the tour of California junior colleges and vocational schools. I took classes as diverse as geography and aviation. I always wanted to fly and thought I should learn a little bit about it, and that led me to taking flying lessons. I took a number of classes on finance, but it was the classes on nutrition, health, and cleansing that were the most interesting to me.

Above all, I was happy to be free. I was ready to create my life the way that I wanted it. And I could do all that here in America. I knew I also needed to learn how to navigate my way around and to get along with my world the way

I saw fit. And I needed to do it in that all-too-American way—all by myself.

My close friend, Muna, the woman who was with me when I slapped the Saudi man with the sandal, was getting married in L.A. I packed my Oldsmobile Omega and headed south. My destination: Los Angeles—the final stop in my long journey to find home.

CHAPTER 7

Getting Settled, Zebiba Style

My trusty Oldsmobile got me all the way to L.A. – barely. It broke down once on the trip, but it got me to where I needed to go next.

It's amusing, really, when you put all of my travels in context of what happens in Africa. In a tribal community, you have many generations living in the same village. Material possessions, because they are so few, are precious, part of the legacy that is passed down. But I was in America now, in the land where it seems everything is disposable, and so I could participate in that other very American tradition of starting completely over.

I chuckle as I look back on this time. I make sure to recycle everything I can, but then I thought it was fantastic that I could use plastic cutlery and paper plates and move on. I could give up my old life, move to a new part of the country, and make something new. If I was feeling good about America before I had that realization, I now fell completely head-over-heels in love with my new adopted country.

I also discovered an interesting phenomenon among immigrants. One or two of us pioneer our way to a new place, and then once we somehow make it safe with our presence, everyone else comes. My first stop in L.A. was Orange County because that's where my friend Muna lived. Now there are many Eritreans living in Orange County, and I probably know the first ones who arrived!

I scheduled my arrival for about a month before Muna's wedding. This wedding was especially dear to me because Muna and I had grown very close, and Nuru, the man she was marrying, happened to be one of my cousins. I focused on this exciting union between two people I cared about very much.

The Thursday before a Saturday wedding, as tradition dictates, the women festoon each other's legs and hands with henna. Made from pulverized plant and sap, henna is combined with lemon and allowed to ferment for a few hours before it is applied to the body. It is a beautiful process. No patterns are used. The astounding, intricate designs all come from the women's creativity. The authentic designs wrap around ankles and up calves, wrists, and arms, and always compliment the body they are being drawn upon.

Women often start their singing and dancing together during this time, in preparation for the celebration of the bride. The closer we got to the actual wedding date, the more serious we got about celebrating. There was dancing and singing throughout the day and far into the night.

Muna and Nuru lived in a huge apartment complex in Cypress (a city in Orange County) after they married. It was almost a village by itself. I was staying with the newlyweds while I put my plan into place: go to college and get a

Chapter 7 • Getting Settled, Zebiba Style

part-time job. After the wedding, I immediately registered at Cypress College. Then I went to the notice board that every college has to look for possible jobs.

My first choice for employment was to serve as a nanny. My English would improve with babysitting; I'd have a place to live, and most of all, I could add to my savings by living rent free. In just a matter of days, there it was: Single Woman with Two Children Seeks Sitter. She actually lived in the same apartment complex I was currently in and was even within walking distance of Muna's place. Even before I phoned, I envisioned that this job would be mine.

A woman named Sarah opened the door. Americans are rarely rude, especially when they are surprised. Sarah was no exception—very gracious. The conversation, pretty quickly, came to references. I talked about the Saudi family and how special their children became to me.

"And I live right over there," I said.

"What do you mean?" Sarah asked.

"Come on, I'll show you," I said. We walked the two sections over to Muna's place.

"Oh, this is the place where the African wedding was happening. Everything smelled so good; people kept coming and going. We noticed that it went on for days after the wedding—," she said with a bemused smile. Needless to say, I got the job.

Sarah's girls had bunk beds. Against the other wall of the same room was mine.

My little home was sublime. The four of us were up at 6 a.m. I'd get the girls to school and then went off to class myself. At 6:00 or 7:00 p.m. when Sarah got home, I would head out and go to my evening classes. Not one of my Eritrean friends could believe the situation I had manifested. I was so close to Muna, I didn't pay rent, and I didn't really have to do much but take the girls back and forth to school. Muna was thrilled that we were neighbors.

I spent a lot of time with those lovely little American girls. They were so much fun, and I was swept up into their spirit.

My obsession with clean homes also came as part of the package. Sarah never, ever considered housekeeping as part of my responsibilities. It was amazing, really. She was a single mother; she trusted me, a stranger from an African country she'd never heard of; I lived in her home and cared for her children. Her kindness and her gratitude made me feel tremendous. I wanted Sarah to walk through the apartment door in the evening and be thrilled at her spotless home. I only know how to do things thoroughly—I've called it "full time," not "part-time." I worked hard for Sarah and her girls, and for the year I was with this family, I felt more like their roommate than a nanny, and I liked that.

As the year progressed, my routine rarely varied. I played with my charges, and I also studied hard to get those college credits. All too soon, my year was over, and it was time to leave. I often wonder what happened to Sarah and her marvelous girls.

After I left my nanny job, I found a nice, kind Eritrean roommate. We rented a two-bedroom apartment. It was lovely. It had a community pool and garden. She had been a Freedom Fighter and was tough as nails. But she was also funny and beautiful and would say the most outrageous things. We would laugh until we cried. She liked to cook. I liked to clean, so that's what we did. I ate very well, and

Chapter 7 • Getting Settled, Zebiba Style

she always had a clean apartment to come home to. It was a beautiful partnership. Our upstairs neighbor wanted to know what we were always laughing about. She even told us she wanted to come live with us!

I was also very busy. I had two jobs and was going full-time to cosmetology school. My roommate was my "model." I always cut her hair, and once I gave her a haircut that everyone, even the beauticians, wanted to copy. One time, I gave her a mohawk and highlighted the tips! Anyone else would have been outraged. Not her. She looked every bit the Freedom Fighter she was.

We would take walks whenever we could. Once, we went for a long walk and as we headed back to our apartment, a guy started following us—flashback to the sandal man in Saudi Arabia. My roommate said, "let's hurry."

I disagreed, "Your cousin lives close. We should go there. "

She said, "What do you mean. I thought you were fearless."

I quickly shot back, "I am fearless, but I'm not stupid fearless. We're going to your cousin's, and he's going to take us home. We don't want that man to know where we live."

She agreed that was the smart thing to do.

Her meals were famous. Everyone, it seemed, found their way to our apartment for a meal at some point. Her cousin and his roommate believed that we were too free-spirited to be traditional. They were sure we didn't know how to cook and clean. They were shocked when they found out we could! He wasn't too sure about us, the cousin's roommate. One time when he was in the hospital, he lied and told the nurse he didn't know who we were. But we had fun anyway.

Building the Impossible: A Refugee's Journey of Giving Back

When I finished cosmetology school, I asked my roommate if she wanted to come with me to do my state board licensing test. She wanted to know if I would have to do something called "press and curl." I said I wasn't sure. I hadn't practiced that a lot. I liked doing cuts and colors, and did that to whomever would let me practice on them. She thought about if for about as second and said, "heck no. I want to keep my hair and my nails." She did find another friend to go with me, and I passed my state boards easily even though I accidently burned my model's ear on the dreaded "press and curl" test.

My roommate always wanted to find a good man and settle down—which she eventually did and now has one set of triplets and one set of twins. But while we were roommates, she kept pestering me about it. "When we leave from this apartment, we're going to move in with our husbands."

I told her, "You might, but I'm going to buy a sports car and move to Santa Monica." And that's exactly what I did. Since I was working two jobs, I saved up enough money to buy a little two-seater. She eventually got her wish and moved in with her husband, a really wonderful man. My brother, Yassin, came to America and stayed in the extra bedroom so that I could help him get established here.

I was definitely living the "better" life that I had chanted for over and over as a child while the Ethiopian soldiers did their deadly work. But I wasn't as happy as I thought I'd be. My heart was still heavy. No matter where I was or what I was doing, I made a point to keep up with what was happening in Eritrea.

The Freedom Fighters never lost heart. They fought valiantly year in and year out so that all Eritreans could be

Chapter 7 • Getting Settled, Zebiba Style

free. It was a noble cause, and we prayed fervently that one day victory would be ours. But the oppression and constant fear I faced as a child was still a way of life in my homeland, and that always tempered how I felt living here in America.

I prayed my homeland would one day be delivered from Ethiopian bonds and the Eritrean people could experience what I had found—independence of thought and freedom of spirit.

Building the Impossible: A Refugee's Journey of Giving Back

Top: Zebiba with Saleh in 2001. Bottom: in 2002, at Saleh's wedding to Amel, when Zebiba surprised him.

Chapter 7 • Getting Settled, Zebiba Style

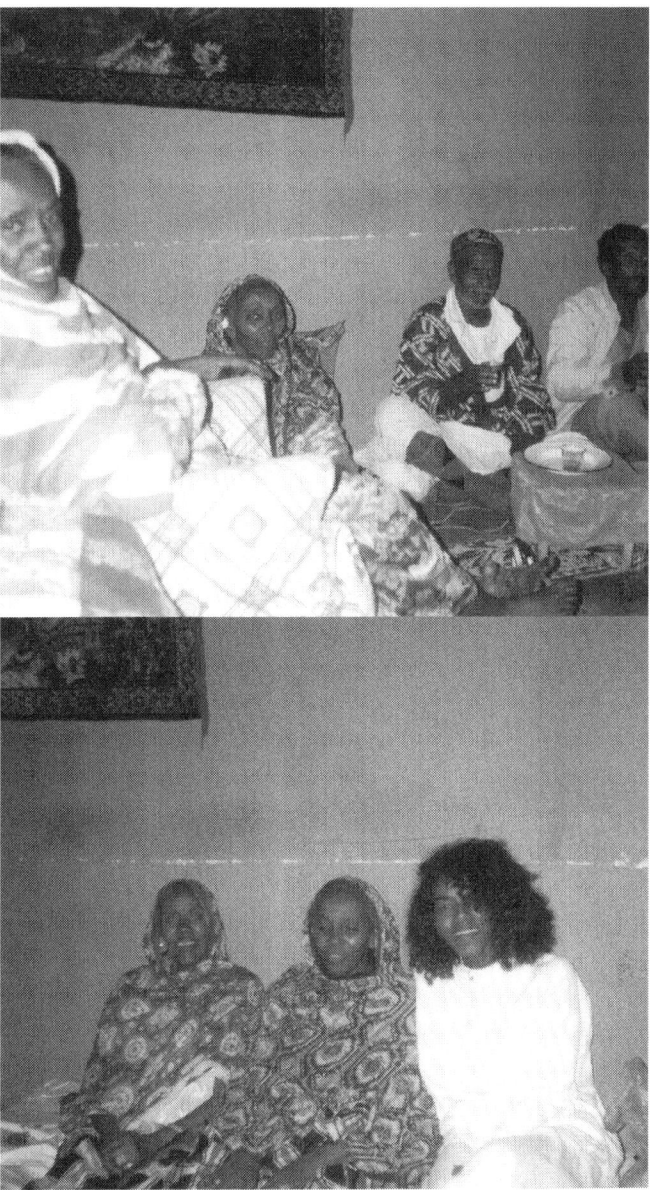

Top: Aunt Nerit, Zebiba's mom, dad, and cousin. Bottom: Aunt Ne'rit, Zebiba's mom, and Zebiba.

Building the Impossible: A Refugee's Journey of Giving Back

Top: Zebiba at Gandhi's house in Gujurat. Bottom: Zebiba at Mother Teresa's memorial site in Calcutta.

Chapter 7 • Getting Settled, Zebiba Style

Top: Zebiba doing yoga. Bottom: Zebiba hiking on Santa Monica Mountain.

Building the Impossible: A Refugee's Journey of Giving Back

Top: Zebiba hiking in Machu Pichu, Peru. Bottom: Zebiba in front of a Mosque in Iran.

Chapter 7 • Getting Settled, Zebiba Style

Top: Zebiba in front a famous restaurant in Vietnam. Bottom: Zebiba in front of a mosque in Saigon.

73

Building the Impossible: A Refugee's Journey of Giving Back

Top: Zebiba with her cousin, Dahab, and her daughter, Ramona, in Sweden.
Bottom: Jackie Kane, Natalie Cole, and Zebiba.

Chapter 7 • Getting Settled, Zebiba Style

Top: Zebiba in front of one of the Great Pyramids in Egypt. Bottom: Zebiba on the Spanish Stairs in Rome.

Building the Impossible: A Refugee's Journey of Giving Back

Top: Saleh on TV in Minnesota talking about the Freedom Fighters. Bottom: Zebiba and Saleh in the Redwood forest in California.

Chapter 7 • Getting Settled, Zebiba Style

Top: Zebiba in the Eritrean lowlands with some locals and a beloved camel.
Bottom: Zebiba's father holding a picture of his brother.

Building the Impossible: A Refugee's Journey of Giving Back

Top: Zebiba with a woman who knew her father. Bottom: Zebiba in front of a hut like she grew up in, in the Eritrean lowlands.

Chapter 7 • Getting Settled, Zebiba Style

Top: Zebiba laughing with Professor Yunus, the founder of the Grameen Bank. Bottom: Lou Walker, Professor Yunus, and Zebiba

Building the Impossible: A Refugee's Journey of Giving Back

Top: Students leaving school at the end of the day. Bottom: The students getting on their bus.

Chapter 7 • Getting Settled, Zebiba Style

Top: In 2008, the students are peeking through the walls of a shack that serves as their school. Bottom: The students of that school gather below with their teacher and Zebiba.

Building the Impossible: A Refugee's Journey of Giving Back

Top: The girls fetching water on a donkey. Bottom: If there is no young girl in the family to handle the chore, the old women go.

Chapter 7 • Getting Settled, Zebiba Style

Top: Zebiba in front of Nelson Mandela's house with the tour guide.
Bottom: Zebiba with her friend, Sue, at Archbishop Desmond Tutu's 70th wedding anniversary event.

Building the Impossible: A Refugee's Journey of Giving Back

Top: Zebiba climbing into a plane to go skydiving, something she can't do anymore, but she's fine with that. Bottom: The apartheid museum in South Africa. It was tough to get through that.

Chapter 7 • Getting Settled, Zebiba Style

Top: Zebiba standing next to Archbishop Desmond Tutu's house in South Africa. Bottom: Zebiba with Jeff MacIntyre, Contact Media, documenting stem-cell therapy in Ecuador.

Building the Impossible: A Refugee's Journey of Giving Back

A little girl in the camps fetching water.

Chapter 7 • Getting Settled, Zebiba Style

Top: Zebiba and Lisa Giannini. Bottom: Megan Orlando, Professor Yunus, and Zebiba.

Building the Impossible: A Refugee's Journey of Giving Back

Zebiba and Dr. Patricia Ross, at a gala, kicking off fundraising for the school.

CHAPTER 8

Eritrean Independence

It finally happened! In 1991, the Eritrean Freedom Fighters won! After over thirty long years of suffering, my birthplace was free from the Ethiopian occupation.

I can only say that it was a true miracle that it occurred in my lifetime. There were celebrations all over the world where Eritreans had settled. We celebrated in people's homes, and there were large scale public celebrations where everyone was invited. The joy we all felt was overwhelming.

Here in America, a group of Eritreans put together the first charter flight back to Eritrea. I would, absolutely, be on that plane, I said to myself. From every state in the continental United States, people flew into Philadelphia where the chartered plane awaited us. It was to be the first plane that landed in Eritrea filled with only Eritreans.

I was returning to see my family and the country we had left behind. It was wonderful to be among a group of human beings, all of whom understood each other's sacrifices up to that point. The singing began as we were taxing out of the airport, and I don't think it ever fully abated through the entire journey back.

Our crew was made up of German men and women who shared our joy. We landed in Frankfurt to refuel, and from there we headed for Eritrea. As it happened, this flight occurred at night, and there still was no electricity in Eritrea. Although there was no military threat of any kind, we couldn't land because it was too dark. The pilot couldn't see!

The newly assembled Eritrean flight control worked with our pilot. Because it was at night and very dark, the captain and crew had to stay tremendously focused. I'm sure it was made even more difficult by the fact that everyone on the plane wanted so badly to be on the ground. The pilot's actions, right in front of us in the cockpit, can only be classified as heroic. He made an emergency landing in Djibouti, a neighboring country also on the Red Sea.

We barely noticed leaving the plane to spend the night in the terminal. We sang and danced the night away, and the hours we had to wait flew by. And the stories—there were things that no one had permitted themselves to even think about for a very long time, stories about the atrocities committed by the Ethiopian soldiers and how the Freedom Fighters started with just seven to ten men. I had grown up knowing about their history because of my Uncle Irdrice. While he was not one of the founding members, he had signed up early on in the fight. We were proud of all our family members who fought so hard to bring us to this momentous occasion.

The next morning we flew into Asmara, exactly as planned. It was the first time in over thirty years that a plane landed safely and officially on Eritrean soil with all of its passenger's passports bearing not a single entry or exit stamp from Ethiopia. As the door was being prepared to open, every one of us stepped back so that the senior members of our charter would be the first ones down the stairs.

Chapter 8 • Eritrean Independence

Hundreds of people jammed the airport. In front of all those who stayed behind—those whom we desperately wanted to hold in our arms—the elder Eritreans got down upon their hands and knees, and with a dignity I shall remember for the rest of my life, kissed the earth beneath them. None of us expected anything that powerful to happen.

During the three weeks that I was there. I traveled to every part of Eritrea that was significant to me. I took my parents to the shore of the Red Sea. My father expressly wanted to bathe in the ocean and soak in the mineral springs there. I took my mom and cousins, and Uncle Irdrice's oldest son also came with us.

I loved being with my family, and I could have spent the entire time vacationing with them, but I knew my trip wouldn't be complete until I felt the warm wind of Tekreret blow through me and again experience its vast open sky.

Muna's sister was a Freedom Fighter, and I met up with her in Massawa, the main port city on the Red Sea. From there, we headed into the desert. As we trekked through the lowlands, our mood sobered considerably. It took forever to get there. As is the case with any war, bridges were blown up and roads destroyed.

More painful for me, however, was the extensive loss of trees. Entire ecosystems were gone. The Freedom Fighters used to hide in the dense jungle, so the Ethiopian soldiers had cut down most of the trees so they could see the movement of the Freedom Fighters better.

I was actually shocked. The Ethiopian government destroyed the infrastructure of the area as well. During the Italian colonization, a train system had been installed connecting Asmara and Massawa. This system of travel no longer existed.

Perhaps most disturbing was the remains of hundreds of bodies. During the war, a multitude of soldiers died on both sides. Since the local villagers no longer had the manpower to bury the carnage, and they couldn't bear the smell, their only choice was to burn the bodies. So as we walked, we also saw everywhere what the fires did not completely burn. The memory of those partially charred bodies haunts me still.

Muna's sister took me to many places in the general lowland area. I didn't know her when I lived in Eritrea, but I recognized in her a kindred spirit—and her son, who was travelling with us, was also an amazing being. I was outraged at the devastation, but because she had fought in the war, Muna's sister was able to put it all in the right perspective. The Freedom Fighters did what was absolutely necessary, and now it was time to rebuild.

I needed to be part of the reconstruction, and there was plenty of that already happening. About twenty minutes from Tekreret, my cousin had a large estate. There were a few huge banana trees still left growing. Their tattered, green leaves now seemed lush. Though a large part of his acreage had been destroyed, this plantation had been successfully maintained by the Freedom Fighters.

I was astounded, really, at how quickly the reconstruction was happening at my cousin's place and all over Eritrea. At that point, I had great hope that Eritrea would regain its proud sense of identity and that the suffering that was still apparent everywhere would soon be gone.

That hope still abides in me, even though the ensuing decades after independence held far more heartache, more

Chapter 8 • Eritrean Independence

even than what the war had inflicted on us. For the destruction that was to happen was caused by our own—and that is always far more devastating.

My trip back to Eritrea also helped me understand what I wanted to do for a career. My trek through the desert reminded me how much I knew about "alternative" healing. Even though, for me, there was nothing "alternative" about it. I grew up using herbs every day. In every Eritrean village and even in the city, when someone caught a cold, they simply chopped a few leaves from the eucalyptus branches right by their house and boiled them. Most of us would then wrap the leaves in a towel and inhale the healing vapors. After that, we'd tuck ourselves under warm blankets in bed and sweat the cold out. The next day we would wake up feeling refreshed and ready to face the day.

We didn't take decongestants or aspirin because we didn't have it. It's actually sad to me. When I went back home in 2001, everyone wanted me to bring over-the-counter medications. I didn't. Instead, I brought back some eucalyptus oil with me. My friends and family laughed at me affectionately, "Oh you are still living in the old days," they'd say. What they probably still don't realize is how much more effective the "old days" are in this case!

When I returned home to L.A., I immediately went searching for classes to help me start my new career. I found a flyer walking along a street in Santa Monica. I signed up for the advertised classes, and after two years of intense study, I was a nutritionist. During this time, I also read as many books as I could about nutrition, cleansing, and fasting. I wanted to know everything I could about my chosen profession. Whenever someone was lecturing on vegetarianism or raw food, I attended. Some of it I thought was completely nuts, too. But I listened anyway looking for some helpful nugget that I could use to help people.

I continue my study in this area to this day. I am always open to learning more about how to keep our bodies strong and lively. I know there's always a more effective way to listen to how our bodies talk to us.

I had also discovered something called The Optimum Health Institute in San Diego, which is all about cleansing and fasting. As part of my extracurricular study, I did their treatments, and I was learning so much. Cleansing, macrobiotics, raw food, I absorbed it all, but I also remembered my early lessons. I realized, quickly, that if the body wasn't cleansed, then all this good food wouldn't really do anything. That sent me into the world of cleansing—sea-weed wraps and other body purification techniques. I knew I had the foundation for what I wanted to do.

I found a place to set up my business in Santa Monica. It was amazing, actually, because it was on the promenade, prime real estate in the area. But because Santa Monica was just "up and coming" when I got there, I was able to rent a room for cheap. My landlord was such a nice woman. She allowed me to put up drywall, paint, and make my nutrition and cleansing boutique my own. I still laugh at the thought of the owners of the coffee shop who would give me free coffee because they thought I was homeless like so many others in the area!

I had learned how to manage a business in health and well-being while I was employed at a spa in Beverly Hills called Acláme. Nerida Joy, the generous and level-headed supervisor, was dedicated to helping whoever walked in

Chapter 8 • Eritrean Independence

the door. Acláme offered everything that could be done to hair, body, fingernails, and toenails. We had makeup people who were pure artists, and we gave facials and treatments for every square inch of the human body. Most importantly, we offered body treatments that were some of the most effective in town. Nutritional counseling was also very popular there. I was assigned to do the seaweed wraps, and it was my introduction into the world of the high-end spa. Eventually, Nerida Joy opened her own very successful clinic in Beverly Hills and has created a line of skin care products that are very popular everywhere. I am proud to know her and thankful for all she taught me.

Finally, after weeks of getting my clinic ready, I was ready to open for business. I called it BodyZAlive, and I am pleased to say that with a lot of hard work and a number of good people who helped me along the way, it flourished. People came from all over to receive the cleansing and nutrition counseling I offered. I was helping people live healthier lives. I was able to support myself, and even save some money.

This last point was important, for while BodyZAlive gave me a career, it was only a stepping stone to putting me back on the path of my mission. Eritrea was always there, always calling, and as the years flew by, my attention kept being pulled to the women and girls in my homeland. They were calling me to help, and I knew that I needed to find a way to go back.

CHAPTER 9

Finding My Purpose

Through my work at BodyZAlive, I was able to meet people who practiced all different religions. I can't think of one religion that wasn't represented by someone who walked through my door. It gave me the best kind of religious education possible. I believe that spirituality is about "beingness," and to grant beingness to both myself and to others. It's about helping others as much as I can. For me, it comes down to choices, and to choose to be helpful, every minute of every day. That is the practice that I follow.

BodyZAlive had grown successful enough that I could afford to travel. Travelling to America as a refugee showed me that travel can open your eyes to different cultures and peoples, but also helps you understand how closely related we are in what we want for ourselves—the freedom to be joyful and to do what we feel is right and good for the world. I enjoyed the people everywhere I went, and I would sometimes go for spiritual retreats. However, every time I went, I couldn't help but see the massive chasm that existed between the "haves" and the "have nots." The people in the non-industrialized parts of the world are startlingly bereft of most of what Americans consider to be necessary for life. It was different than the way I grew up. My tribal upbringing had existed for thousands of years. But when I visited a posh retreat high on a hill in a third-world country, I had a stark wake-up call. At the bottom there was a squalid village of people barely subsisting in shacks that were scarcely held together let alone offer any real protection from the elements. It disturbed me when I stopped to really look at the whole situation.

Once again I thought of the women and girls in the refugee camps. I was living a "good" life—full of freedom, good food, a warm bed to sleep in. It was easy to get caught up in the "everyday" drama that comes with just living. But what about these women who sometimes didn't eat for a few days so their children had their daily rations? What about the girls? They weren't going to school. I knew that they were getting married younger and younger because there wasn't any other way for the parents to support them. But that meant they were having babies at a younger and younger age. That presented health problems of magnitude, for both the infant and the mother.

As I travelled the world, I found that my heart was leading me down a path that I knew would be difficult, even painful sometimes, but one that I knew would ultimately bring me spiritual joy.

When I visited Eritrea in 1991, especially the villages, I always felt a pang of guilt for having a blessed life in America. There is so much abundance that exists in such visible ways, I couldn't help but want to do much more. But I also realized that America and its people are so open, so willing to help those who need it. People in America exhibit a "heart" that I never found anywhere else. I also noticed something as I travelled: the government of a country

Chapter 9 • Finding My Purpose

makes a difference. When people emphasize communist or socialist ways of living, the people aren't as open. It seems harder for them to survive, so they aren't as willing to give of themselves. I wanted to be able to help others just as the Catholic charity in Italy had helped me and thousands of other refugees on our respective journeys.

In 1993, Eritrea held a referendum. According to U.N. rules, the country had to vote to make their separation from Ethiopia official. It was also the referendum that made Isaias Afwerki (the Eritreans call him simply Isaias, according to their custom) the declared first "head of state."

Eritreans across the globe were asked to vote on the final step of legitimization of Eritrean independence. The referendum won by a landslide. We were all excited, but then I heard the news that the Jehovah Witnesses weren't voting for religious reasons. They had been persecuted, imprisoned, harassed, and tortured.

Shortly after the referendum, it became obvious that Isaias was not interested in honoring the fundamental human rights of Eritreans, especially the freedom of speech. And sure enough, the farther we got away from the year of Eritrean independence, the worse Isaias became.

Even though Eritreans were supposed to be enjoying the fruits of independence, reports were leaking out that all was not well. Eritrea had declared war on Ethiopia soon after independence in '91 over some sort of border dispute. The Eritrean government, run by the head of the Eritrean People's Liberation Front (the EPLF) had instituted mandatory military service—for *every* "able bodied" Eritrean. This service was supposed to last only eighteen months, but in fact the length of conscription, the stories whispered, was taking years.

There were also more reports of rape, beatings, and all manner of other human rights abuses inside and outside of these mandatory military encampments.

While all the torture and abuse was going on in Eritrea, I was trying to figure out a way to help. I was working hard and continued travelling, hoping to find the right angle to help as I observed people living in other third-world countries.

On one of my trips, I got lost in the jungle in Costa Rica. I walked for miles, and it reminded me of Tekreret. I was fortunate enough to find a farmer to help me, but my experience there touched me deeply. As I returned to America, I felt in the core of my being that I hadn't done much, that I could do a great deal more.

My brother Saleh had found a way to directly help our homeland. When he returned to Eritrea after the referendum, Isaias named him Minister of Fisheries and Marine Resources and then the Minister of Health.

If I didn't do something, then I was no better than those who had a bad habit of just talking a lot about their "pet cause," but not doing much of anything to actually help.

In the last years of the 1990s, I formulated a plan. I would work for the next few years building BodyZalive into a thriving business so that I could sell it. As I worked, I couldn't help but notice that while there is much goodness in the world, there is also the opposite. It is amazing to me how some human beings will find any way possible to torture each other. I was becoming overwhelmed with the continual escalation of suffering in the world until, finally,

Chapter 9 • Finding My Purpose

it hit me. The world separates people, if not by race then by religion; if not by ethnicity then by gender. Either it is a tribal thing, or a caste system thing, but it always seems to come down to some version of "us" versus "them." And this isn't something that is reserved for only the poorest countries on the planet. But all of these separations, the dividing of humans into skin color or belief, is damaging to the human spirit.

As the world suffered through more strife, I looked around and felt that this was no way for the world to live, and I decided that it was now time to really start doing something about it. I could no longer sit back and watch the events of the world escalate into more hatred and more terror. I saw this as an opportunity to lift others and myself to another level where honest communication could result.

I took my inspiration from Argentina. Here was a people who had endured civil war, just like I had, and they had their hero. Eva Peron's legacy of humanitarianism is everywhere present in her country. She championed the working class, and that left a far more powerful and effective legacy than western history has ever recorded. Her real history touched my heart deeply. It re-established my faith in the power of human ingenuity, in the value of living simply and using, not abusing, what the good earth gives you. It breathed a feeling of hope in me that I really could bring back that spirit to my birthplace that had been so worn down by too many years of war and its aftermath. I was ready to go to my homeland again, to bring to my countrymen all of what I had, my sense of freedom, my love of being independent, and my ability to help.

In 2002, I knew it was time to sell my beloved clinic. This turned out to be actually very easy. I had set my sights on a particular client who had started coming to BodyZalive when I first opened. Over the years, we became close friends. Once the word was out regarding the availability of my business for sale, many generous and exciting offers were made, but I knew that this particular friend would have a natural knack for it. I offered the clinic to her, and there was not even a hint of hesitation in the tone of her voice when she accepted. We agreed on the terms of purchase and she bought the business. I am pleased to note that BodyZalive is doing well under the steerage of this dear friend.

I now had the funds and the time to start truly making my dream real. I decided I was going to help the women and children in Eritrea. I had no idea what I was in for.

Chapter 9 • Finding My Purpose

makes a difference. When people emphasize communist or socialist ways of living, the people aren't as open. It seems harder for them to survive, so they aren't as willing to give of themselves. I wanted to be able to help others just as the Catholic charity in Italy had helped me and thousands of other refugees on our respective journeys.

In 1993, Eritrea held a referendum. According to U.N. rules, the country had to vote to make their separation from Ethiopia official. It was also the referendum that made Isaias Afwerki (the Eritreans call him simply Isaias, according to their custom) the declared first "head of state."

Eritreans across the globe were asked to vote on the final step of legitimization of Eritrean independence. The referendum won by a landslide. We were all excited, but then I heard the news that the Jehovah Witnesses weren't voting for religious reasons. They had been persecuted, imprisoned, harassed, and tortured.

Shortly after the referendum, it became obvious that Isaias was not interested in honoring the fundamental human rights of Eritreans, especially the freedom of speech. And sure enough, the farther we got away from the year of Eritrean independence, the worse Isaias became.

Even though Eritreans were supposed to be enjoying the fruits of independence, reports were leaking out that all was not well. Eritrea had declared war on Ethiopia soon after independence in '91 over some sort of border dispute. The Eritrean government, run by the head of the Eritrean People's Liberation Front (the EPLF) had instituted mandatory military service—for *every* "able bodied" Eritrean. This service was supposed to last only eighteen months, but in fact the length of conscription, the stories whispered, was taking years.

There were also more reports of rape, beatings, and all manner of other human rights abuses inside and outside of these mandatory military encampments.

While all the torture and abuse was going on in Eritrea, I was trying to figure out a way to help. I was working hard and continued travelling, hoping to find the right angle to help as I observed people living in other third-world countries.

On one of my trips, I got lost in the jungle in Costa Rica. I walked for miles, and it reminded me of Tekreret. I was fortunate enough to find a farmer to help me, but my experience there touched me deeply. As I returned to America, I felt in the core of my being that I hadn't done much, that I could do a great deal more.

My brother Saleh had found a way to directly help our homeland. When he returned to Eritrea after the referendum, Isaias named him Minister of Fisheries and Marine Resources and then the Minister of Health.

If I didn't do something, then I was no better than those who had a bad habit of just talking a lot about their "pet cause," but not doing much of anything to actually help.

In the last years of the 1990s, I formulated a plan. I would work for the next few years building BodyZalive into a thriving business so that I could sell it. As I worked, I couldn't help but notice that while there is much goodness in the world, there is also the opposite. It is amazing to me how some human beings will find any way possible to torture each other. I was becoming overwhelmed with the continual escalation of suffering in the world until, finally,

CHAPTER 10

A Destroyed Homeland

I travelled back to Eritrea in 2001 for a second time, and it was wonderful to see my family. I knew the war had widowed many women and orphaned far too many children—many of whom had to fend for themselves—and I was deeply disturbed by what I saw.

But I was also shocked at what had happened in my country since that wonderful year of independence. Basically, Isaias had instituted a communist government. Everything felt restricted. I remember asking some of those who had governmental power what was going on, and they would say, in all seriousness, "there's too much freedom in America" or even in Europe, and "people in Eritrea don't need that much freedom." My brother, Saleh, who was at that point the Minister of Health, even said this to me.

Isaias had also made it so he did not have to answer to anyone. It took three years, from 1994 to 1997, for the Eritrean constitution to be ratified. It called for legislative, executive, and judicial branches of government, with a unicameral (meaning one party) National Assembly that was supposed to decide internal and external policy, approve the budget, and elect the president of the country. It was beautiful on paper, but it was never implemented.

As I pointed out, at that time, Isaias was elected "Head of State," and Eritrean national elections were supposed to happen in 1997. But those never happened either. Isaias used a border conflict between Eritrea and Ethiopia as a pretext to keep the elections from happening and the constitution from being implemented.

Another national election was scheduled for December of 2001, but it was postponed *indefinitely*—for no reason. The National Assembly has not met since 2002. Legislative as well as executive functions are now exercised exclusively by President Isaias Afwerki. There is no rule of law, and Isaias is now a fully totalitarian dictator wreaking havoc on the people of Eritrea.

In 2001, Eritrea had been "independent" for a decade. Once the war in Eritrea ended and it became a sovereign country, and after the United Nations had organized the referendum for the Eritreans to decide their future, the UN also prepared a program to repatriate the refugees from the camps to the areas of their origin.

The Office of the UN High Commissioner prepared a program of resettling the refugees back to their homeland in peace, security, dignity, and assistance in accordance with the international standard for returnees.

Unfortunately, the newly established Eritrean Government consistently sabotaged and obstructed the efforts of the international community to assist the Eritrean refugees to return from Sudan. It was evident that the Eritrean government was not keen for its citizens to return to their homeland. But because the refugees were unable to go back to Eritrea, and the U.N. was unable to help them further, this is when they became "forgotten."

Chapter 10 • A Destroyed Homeland

My visit in 2001 was difficult, but before I left Eritrea, I knew I had one more person to see. My Aunt Ne'rit was still alive. She had moved back to the Eritrean lowlands following the death of her husband in Sudan. I asked everyone to keep my arrival a secret from her, so it was wonderful to see the look of surprise and then pure pleasure when she saw me. I spent a few days with her, and we made the journey back to my beloved Tekreret.

When we got there, Aunt Ne'rit and I searched for where we remembered my family's hut, or at least its foundation, to be. Another family friend who was present at my birth took us to the spot. It didn't take her very long. She was positive and pointed. "Remember when you would sit at the base of this tree? This was how we found your hut from all the others, when we'd visit."

Though it had been chopped to its very base, the roots of this ancient tree were extensive and indestructible. It struck me as beautifully poetic. The courageous remains of this tree were the final marker of where I was conceived. Its roots were my roots—and neither could ever be wrenched completely from this soil.

We took it all in. We walked around a bit more, cried, took pictures, and in typical Eritrean fashion, we moved on.

As I left Tekreret that second time, it was odd. I felt like my childhood had been all-but erased, that in one sense my old self had died. But even with all that, I didn't feel empty. I knew that in my new homeland, I had found so many of the good things that I had lost here in this little patch of earth.

As I walked out of that place, I felt a strong sense of purpose. My childhood was now more precious to me because its outer trappings had been wiped away. I wanted more than anything else for the children of Eritrea, the ones who had survived the war orphaned and hungry, to be able to feel the joy and wonder of being a child. I decided then and there that for the rest of my life, I would dedicate myself to the children. For it is in childhood that a person learns to both give and receive. If you don't have that, then what do you have?

The last few days of that trip, I spent in Asmara. I was determined to find a way to help, but I hit wall after wall—it seemed "help" was impossible in this regime. I left Asmara broken-hearted and confused. What was I going to do?

CHAPTER 11

The Atrocities

I knew it was getting increasingly worse in Eritrea. Around the time I was visiting my Aunt Ne'rit, an open letter was published by a group called the "G-15." The letter appeared in May, 2001, and it confirmed the rumors.

"G-15" stands for a group of fifteen senior officials that included Eritrean senior cabinet ministers, former Freedom Fighters who now worked directly with Isaias, as well as generals, and members of parliament, all of whom were also members of the ruling party (the PFDJ).

They came to oppose President Afwerki after the disastrous border war with Ethiopia, questioning him on how he ran the war and the nation. Together, they signed that open letter criticizing his authoritarian rule and demanding democratic reform; they specifically stressed the full implementation of the ratified constitution.

Their names are: Beraki Gebreselassire, Ogbe Abraha, Haile Woldetensae, Petros Solomon, Mahmoud Ahmed Sherifo, Berhane Gebregziabher, Saleh Idris Kekia, Estefanos Seyoum, Germano Nati, Mesfin Hagos, Hamid Himid, Aster Fesehazion, Mehamed Berhan Blata, Adhanom Gebremariam, and Mahmoud Ahmed.

Building the Impossible: A Refugee's Journey of Giving Back

In September of 2001, Isaias's regime arrested eleven members of the G-15. Three others were outside the country and one had already recanted. Even though never officially charged in a court of law, the Eritrean government claimed that they were guilty of defeatism, conspiracy to unseat the president, and treason.

In the seventeen years (as of the publication of this book) that they have been detained, the Eritrean government has held them incommunicado and refused to tell their whereabouts or health condition or even whether they are alive or dead. Other news has been coming out from other informal sources, and it is not good.

In 2011, a former prison guard in Eraero Prison in Eritrea by the name of Eyob Bahta, who successfully made his way to Ethiopia, said that six of them had already died (former vice president Mahmoud Sherifo, military chief of staff Ogbe Abraha, and central committee members Aster Fisehatsion, Germano Nati, Hamid Himid and Salih Kekya) and the rest were in dire health condition (the former foreign minister Haile Woldetensae had lost his sight).[2]

In September, 2001, there was also another group that faced the same fate as the eleven of the G-15, the independent journalists. In an unprecedented attack on the free press, seven of the country's independent newspapers were shut down and within a week ten journalists were arrested (Yusuf Mohamed Ali, Seyoum Tsehaye, Dawit Isaak, Temesgen Gebreyesus, Mattewos Habteab, Dawit Habtemichael, Medhanie Haile, Fessehaye Yohannes, Said Abdulkadir and Amanuel Asrat), with more following in the next month.

[2] Interview with Eyob Banta – Part 1 (Video). 4 January, 2011.
http://www.asmarino.com/interviews/1182-interview-with-eyob-bahta-english-version

Chapter 11 • The Atrocities

Again, they were not formally charged, but the government accused them of being a national security threat, working as agents for foreign NGOs, etc. And as was the case of the eleven arrested from the G-15, the journalists have been held incommunicado ever since. Among the seventeen journalists held in prison, some are presumed dead.

The former guard also mentioned five journalists who died in the same prison camp, one from suicide and the rest from harsh prison conditions. (Mattewos Habteab, Temesgen Gebreyesus, Saleh Tsegazab are among those mentioned). Another four from the 2001 arrestees—Medhanie Haile, Yusuf Mohamed Ali, Said Abdulkader and Fessehaye "Joshua" Yohannes—are also believed to have died in detention.

The arrests of the G-15 members and the journalists were part of a full-blown effort to suppress political dissent nationwide; since then the totalitarian grip over the population has been growing tighter and tighter. In the decade and half since their arrest, forced disappearances, arbitrary arrests, mass detentions, torture, military roundups, and other crimes against humanity, have been used to stifle any kind of dissent or opposition.

When I said in the previous chapter that Isaias is a totalitarian dictator, this is what I mean: no opposition parties are allowed; independent journalism is nonexistent; the judiciary system doesn't function; and civic groups are not allowed. Freedom of expression, movement, assembly, worship, and association are all banned. There is not even a glimmer of a national election on the horizon. The only ruling party allowed is that of the PFDJ, and even that is answerable only to Isaias.

Building the Impossible: A Refugee's Journey of Giving Back

Since Eritrean independence, 314 prison and detention camps have been built to house the thousands of dissenters, military deserters, and conscription evaders. To put this into even starker perspective, the only university that existed in Eritrea was shut down permanently by the regime. To add insult to injury, the indefinite national service created by Isaias to "build" his military in fact still traps tens of thousands of youth in military camps. This has turned the nation into the biggest open prison in the world.

The result is a totalitarian horror, documented by the U.N. and other human rights organizations such as Amnesty International. The 2016 report of the U.N. Commission Inquiry on Eritrea specifically says, "The 2001 clampdown set in motion a chain of egregious, widespread and systematic human rights violations that continues to this very day, including arbitrary arrests, incommunicado detention, denial of the right to a fair trial within a reasonable time," as well as stories of rape, torture, and enforced labor that should be called slavery.[3]

As 2001 ended, I knew I would be walking into a wasp's nest if I went back to Eritrea, but I was compelled to return. I knew if I looked hard enough, I could find a way to positively impact those remaining in Eritrea, even in the face of these ever-mounting human rights atrocities.

---

3 "Eritrea: 15 years later still no information on jailed senior politicians and independent journalists. Huan Hantions Human Rights Office of the High Commissioner. 16 September, 2016. http://www.ohchr.org/EN/NewsEvents/Pages/DisplayNews.aspx?NewsID=20515&LangID=E.

See also. Human Rights Watch. World Report, 2015. https://www.hrw.org/sites/default/files/reports/wr2015.pdf

CHAPTER 12

Finding Possibilities

I made plans for a trip in 2002, which had a dual purpose: I wanted to help my father who was aging and his health was starting to fail, but I also wanted to find out if my other plans to help Eritrea would work.

From 2001 to 2002, I had been busy, making inquiries into various organizations who could possibly help in Eritrea, from solar power to clean water to group homes and microfinancing. I found group homes promising—four or five children live with one adult, preferably a mother who herself had a number of children. That would offer the orphaned children more of a family and thus more support than an orphanage-type of situation.

However, it was micro-loans that intrigued me most. I remember vividly a woman I met on the bus in 2001. We were in between the lowlands and Asmara. She was beautiful—cleanly dressed in her white muslin wrap and carrying a huge bowl full of eggs. I asked her what the eggs were for. She told me she sells them. I bought her entire inventory, and she was truly grateful.

I always made a point to buy vegetables or whatever goods women were selling on city corners wherever I was in Eritrea. And I was always struck by something. These women were finding ways to support themselves, and when they did, no matter how much or how little they sold, I never saw despair in their eyes. It gave me the idea that if all the mothers could have access to enough funds to start their own businesses, then they could support themselves and make enough money for their children to go to school.

Shortly after I returned from Eritrea in 2001, I had discovered the work of Professor Yunus, an economics professor who founded the Grameen Bank in 1976 in Bangladesh, his homeland. It was set up specifically to give microloans to women in developing countries to start small home-based businesses as a way of supporting themselves. He won a Nobel Peace prize in 2006 for his work.

I was ecstatic. This could offer real help. I was reminded of the old proverb: "Give a man fish and he eats for a day. Teach him to fish and he eats for a lifetime." Instead of just giving my country-women some "fish" to eat, I would be giving them a way to start a "fishing business," that would give them the wherewithal they needed to make sure their children were educated.

I started formulating a plan. I would set up a micro-lending funding system as a way to help Eritrean women set up their own businesses just like the micro-credit programs that were working in Bangladesh. It was such a beautiful system. A woman creates a business around her talents. African women might not be educated in ways that we think of in the West, but they have incredibly valuable skills. Their talents are in their hands—their skills are in weaving, farming, and organizing. Eritrean women, for example, make all sorts of wonderful things, from baskets to amazing woven textiles, to beautiful embroidery on the

Chapter 12 • Finding Possibilities

clothes they wear—and they don't even use a pattern. It's just created straight out of their imaginations and their wonderfully skilled hands.

The beauty of a micro-loan program, I found, was it didn't matter if a woman was good at knitting or at farming, she could support her family in some small, sustainable way using that skill. I decided that I wanted to see all of my Eritrean sisters self-sustained and self-contained. At that time, many women were already running their own life, so tending after their own successful business would give them so much more. Through micro loans, I could offer these women a way out of poverty, so they could raise their children with dignity.

I wasn't able to make any headway during that 2002 trip. I was still getting stopped at every turn by the government. But I had hope because when I arrived the fall of that year, Isaias's regime seemed very shaky and didn't appear to be lasting. I thought, "Great. I'll do what I can on this trip and then come back in a year and just start."

I left Eritrea, a woman on a mission. I needed to see for myself how these micro-loan programs were being handled in other countries. I left Eritrea the way I always ended my trips back home, "Hopefully next time I come, Eritrea will have a new leader that will allow me to help and is dedicated to rebuilding the country."

I embarked on a two-year tour of Asia, and I knew where I had to go first—a place that has adopted micro-lending with gusto and has major success with it: India.

India is immense—and is populated by an unbelievable amount of people. Enormous numbers of men, women, and children crowd the cities and towns. It brought a very vivid quote by Charles Dickens to mind: "It was the best of times; it was the worst of times."

I spent six months in India. I explored it all, the big cities and the small towns. Everywhere I went, I saw evidence of the micro-loan program working. In India and Bangladesh, the fine art of hand-beading is flourishing and very much part of the micro-loan program. The women bead in their homes and then someone comes and pays them for their work.

I learned that the recipient was loaned enough money to start their business, whether that was to buy a cow or a cell phone. Then, because the loans came with a very low interest rate, the women could pay it back while still building their own economic base. It did wonders for the stability of these women.

What I liked best about the micro-loan program—and still do— was that it doesn't dictate to the recipient what she must do. Rather, it allows her to take her best skill and capitalize on it. I thought maybe micro lending could skirt the government restrictions on giving money directly to these needy women. I was thrilled.

India, I am also very glad to say, also offered me something else, something that touched me personally, and like South America, reminded me of the deeper reason why I was doing this work. I traveled to Calcutta and then to Gujarat, the homes of India's two great spiritual leaders, Mother Theresa and Mahatma Gandhi, respectively. At Mother Theresa's convent and Gandhi's home, I was struck by how simply they lived. Mother's Theresa's tomb is much larger than her room. What she wore and what she ate

Chapter 12 • Finding Possibilities

reminded me, again, of how I grew up. One doesn't need a lot of material goods to live a full life.

At Gandhi's home in Gujarat, I was touched, profoundly, to see his room, the bowls and actual spoons he ate with, where he made his speeches and the very tree he sat beneath and meditated. He wanted peace in India, an India free of any religious oppression or colonization. His wish for India matched my wish for Eritrea, and I was inspired by his willingness to give everything he had to accomplish his mission.

In Bangalore, a very surprising trio crossed my path, literally. One of the gentlemen was from Sierra Leone, a country in West Africa. The other two men were from Afghanistan. I was sitting at a table next to them one morning at breakfast, and I found out that they had just completed a seminar on farming where they were invited participants. They were going back to Afghanistan, and I was intrigued. I introduced myself to them, and we talked about many different topics besides farming. As it turned out, the African gentleman was an employee of the United Nations. He was stationed in Afghanistan and promptly gave me his card. "Come visit Afghanistan," he said.

"I will," I replied. About two weeks after that, I made the call and was on my way to visit this country in the throes of war.

I must be a nomad at heart because I can't keep a travel itinerary to save my life. I made it to Afghanistan without a problem, and as I was being driven to my hotel, I was instantly transported back to Eritrea, both in the lowlands and in the city. It was 2003, and Afghanistan was nothing but a vast war zone. The buildings were bombed out, and the hotel constantly issued warnings to not travel. Being in Afghanistan during that time made me remember things from my childhood that I thought were buried forever. I had hoped that I would never have to feel the raw fear that comes with hearing tanks shooting at each other or bombs going off too close to your home. It's a fear that makes you freeze because there is no place to go.

It was an eerie feeling, to say the least, to have to stay in my hotel to remain safe, but when I was able to venture out and travel locally, I met as many Afghanis as I could. Meeting the people of Afghanistan affected me more deeply than any other people in any other country I have been to. They reminded me of the Eritrean people, strong spirits and strong-minded. Their resolution to rebuild their country is the finest example of determination on earth. The look in their eyes, the way they calmly went about the business of reconstruction, reminded me in a way nothing else could of the brave men and women who had given their lives so that Eritrea could have its independence.

The women and men who are there now are going about their own business of cleaning up after a war. I do not have a word for the amazing nature of determination of the Afghani people. Though my time there was brief, the Afghanis left me speechless.

From Afghanistan, I traveled to Thailand and Laos. Both countries are full of richness, whether it is in Thai silks or Laotian culture. From there I went on to Vietnam. After what I witnessed in Afghanistan, I was curious to see for myself how the Vietnamese have dealt with the aftermath of their war. As I worked my way through Vietnam, I could

Chapter 12 • Finding Possibilities

still see its people struggling with the after-effects of the "Vietnam War" that had ended over thirty years ago.

I visited the museum and was shocked at what I saw. There were stories and pictures of babies born with two heads, or four legs, or three eyes or one, all because of Agent Orange. What struck me most, however, is how forgiving and even welcoming the Vietnamese are of the West. Their forgiveness for the past really moved me. They are moving on and creating their lives over again, and suddenly it hit me. Even though I will never forget what happened, I could find it in my heart to forgive the Ethiopian soldiers for what they did to the women and children and for burning the villages.

South America had brought me back to the Tekreret of my childhood when I could still feel the freedom of the wind in the trees, experience the richness of all that life promised. South East Asia had me revisit the war that I lived through, made me face squarely the tragic destitution that war always leaves, the destitution that I never had to fully deal with because I had left Eritrea and gone to America. And as I went through the whole progression of my life in my mind, my mission started to become clearer and clearer. Recharged from my epiphany in Vietnam, I ventured into Malaysia and then Indonesia, and there, my education into the real heart of my mission continued. What struck me about Malaysia was that it has an astounding variety of ethnic races that are all collaborating. There is not the "us" versus "them" attitude that I find so prevalent in so many places. All these ethnicities working together are a marvel. Then, what I found in Indonesia was astounding.

Indonesia is predominately a Muslim country, but instead of shutting down and even persecuting other religions, it seemed to me that the Indonesian government had adopted tolerance for all faiths. My father instilled in me the firm belief that everyone has the right to practice their own customs, traditions, and religion. But seeing the effects of an active, living tolerance in Indonesia helped me to see that the only way that we humans will stop torturing each other is by accepting our differences.

I had planned on visiting Bali last. I loved Bali. It is 83 percent Balinese Hindu, and the government lets everyone practice their belief—much like the rest of Indonesia. Bali also was the only really selfish part of my Asian trip. I knew that I would need to rest, and what a better place to do it than one of the true paradises on earth. I found a shack on the beach, and I was very content to jog or walk on the gorgeous sand. The Balinese woman managing the place thought that I needed to be social, however, so she was constantly inviting me to a different party or to go to other "cool" places during the day, every day.

On one particular night, my hostess had invited me to a restaurant opening. I liked attending parties with her. I met a lot of really amazing people that way, and it broke me out of my routine of running on the beach at 5:00 a.m. and then going back for a walk at sunset. But on the evening of the restaurant opening, of all nights, I was ready to do something else. I had met a wonderful family from Australia at my hotel, and I was having dinner with them. There was a woman, Jane, her son John, and a man whom I thought was her husband. His name was Win. This night at dinner, I was sitting across from him, and that's when

Chapter 12 • Finding Possibilities

I found out that he was Jane's brother, not her husband. He was fascinating, and I could immediately tell he was a beautiful being all the way through.

And...he wasn't Jane's husband.

Well, *okay*. Here he was, the man I had always dreamed about. I had been praying that, during all of my travels, I wouldn't fall in love.

The evening was magical. I had a beautiful view of the pool and the ocean beyond that. I was enthralled and loved watching this family interact. And there was Win.

Win and I did not part after that evening. On that first night, we spoke for hours. I found out that he believes in living simply and that he too has a purpose to help people. I spent the rest of my vacation with him, traveling around the island.

He lived in Bali, but he convinced me to travel to Australia and meet his family. I met his father first and then we drove cross-country to meet and stay with his mother. On the way to his mom's house, Win surfed and I walked. I enjoyed everything, from the way the sand felt between my toes to the strong Australian sun.

We stopped in many towns and cities. I have fallen in love before, but this one was unlike anything else I had experienced. Win is one of the kindest human beings I have ever met, a peaceful, gentle man. I was deeply, truly, in love. I also experienced for the first time what it felt like to be deeply loved by a man with no conditions and with no restrictions. We were so much alike in important ways, yet different enough to keep it all new and exciting. I thought, "I can surely handle this one."

But even though I was in that wonderfully luscious and timeless space of new love, I couldn't forget all that I had learned on my year-and-a-half journey around the world. I also certainly couldn't forget the hell my country-women were experiencing daily, wondering how they were going to get enough food to feed their large families let alone having even one of their children go to school. I had to honor that purpose.

I had a choice to make, and it was a true test of my code of staying true to me. I love the experience of this life. I have always felt that this world is one planet on which all of us can live peacefully if we work at it. I do not see lines of color and languages as barriers. It is one planet, and we have to travel upon it, experience its corners, and accept our differences. I can't see the difference between Africa or America, between Asia and South America. Each region calls me. While I am alive, I will try to experience every country and listen to every language that is spoken. At the same time, I feel compelled to help.

I knew what I had to do. Win was a wonderful free spirited human being, but my purpose was to work with the women and children in Eritrea. Win went back to Bali, and I returned briefly to the U.S. to prepare for my next trip to Eritrea.

CHAPTER 13

The Astounding Truth

I arrived for my visit in 2006. The situation in Eritrea had worsened considerably since I had been there three years prior. This saddened me to no end.

When everyone banded together as Freedom Fighters, they took care of each other. They were like a family. But the farther away from independence Eritrea got, the more the leaders were doing the exact opposite. There wasn't enough food. Those in the national service were being abused emotionally, physically, even sexually. It was almost too much. But all I could think about were the children. Were they getting enough food and clean water? Were they being educated?

When I got to Asmara, I decided I would interview families and find out who needed help. I had tried doing this during earlier trips but was quickly stopped by the government. This time, I decided I would have the government's blessing.

I visited my brother, Saleh, right away. I wanted him to help me put my plan into action. He was still holding his post as Minister of Health, but after fifteen years of Isaias's abusive dictatorship, I could tell that he felt utterly discontent. He had left his life in America to help Isaias rebuild

Eritrea, but he intimated to me that he felt used, that Isaias wasn't a leader. He was a totalitarian despot who had no intention of instituting any rule of law let alone reforms that would move Eritrea forward as a country.

I told Saleh my plan. He knew he couldn't stop me, so my beloved brother looked me dead in the eye and said, emphatically, "I don't think this is going to work, Zebiba, but I know what drives you. You want to help your country, just as I did. I know that I am a marked man. I don't worship Isaias. I don't say and do everything he wants. But I'm not going to leave the country; he either puts me in jail or he will kill me, but I came to serve the Eritrean people, and that's what I will continue to do."

I knew exactly what he was talking about. I knew about the containers of medicine that Saleh had secured for Eritrea but that sat in the Red Sea port of Massawa until it had gone bad. That frustrated my brother to no end. "Why am I doing my job?" he would ask, seemingly to no one in particular. The G-15 were all presumed dead even though their families still didn't know what happened. We were all surprised that Saleh had lived this long.

But even though he thought my idea to interview families was a fool's errand, he also knew me well enough to know that I wouldn't stop until I found a way into the schools to interview parents, principals, and even the students. Saleh sent me to the Minister of Education, whom I met with right away. I told this Minister which schools I wanted to visit, and he approved.

When I first arrived in Asmara, I went directly to one of the poorest schools in the city. I heard most of the students were children of Freedom Fighters who had lost their

Chapter 13 • The Astounding Truth

parents. Those who took them in—their grandparents or aunts and uncles—didn't have much to begin with. They also had children of their own, but that didn't matter. The parents of these orphans had given their lives for Eritrea, so these generous, selfless people took their children and raised them as their own.

I went to the principal of the school and asked for about a hundred kids to profile. What I found was that there were four, five, or more children in just one family, barely surviving. These surrogate parents barely had enough money to cover the cost of food and other essentials let alone all the school supplies the parents had to fund (which, I found out, was everything.) I decided that to be fair, I would sponsor a child from each family, no matter how many kids each family had. I chose a hundred kids from the inner city of Asmara and a hundred kids from the lowlands. There were thousands more who needed help, but I had to start somewhere.

After I had gathered my information, I was excited. The parents were excited as were the schools. I fully expected that I could start helping the parents and the schools quickly.

I went back to the Minister of Education who respectfully listened to my proposal. And then told me, "I can't help you."

I didn't understand. I had taken the students' profiles. I knew who I wanted to send money to. The Minister said that I couldn't send money directly to the schools to help the children. I had to send it to the government who would then give it to the schools they thought worthy. I would have absolutely no control over the outcome. I knew that if I sent money to the government, very little if *any* would make it into the hands of the mothers.

I was furious, not at the Minister but at their policy. If it were only the decision of this Minister that I met, I would have trusted him fully. But I knew the decision wasn't ultimately in his hands. He was following orders, and I had no recourse.

"That's absolutely unacceptable," I screamed at Saleh when I went back and told him what happened.

Saleh's only response was a warning because he knew I was going to do *something*. "Don't make too much noise. If something happened, I couldn't help you."

I could see in his eyes that something was going on, but I knew better than to ask. I knew he couldn't tell me anything anyway. That incensed me even more. What was *really* going on, and how could I possibly be in any danger? All I wanted to do was help Eritrean children get educated. Maybe all the rumors were true. God forbid.

Then Saleh said something interesting. "There's nothing you can do here. Go to the refugee camps and help them." This made me pause. The official stance concerning the refugees—then and now—was denial through silence. Everyone knew Eritreans were fleeing the country in droves, but Isaias lied and said it wasn't happening.

I walked around Asmara, wondering if I just needed to give up. This was the third time I had travelled back Eritrea, hoping to do something for the women and children. I thought of all that I had done, for example introducing Medicine for Humanity to my brother. This is a group of doctors from UCLA and John Hopkins, as well as their interns and nurses, who travel to African countries to

Chapter 13 • The Astounding Truth

help women suffering from female maladies ranging from cervical cancer to urinary fistula. The latter is the result of prolonged labor that causes bladder leakage, and while it is an entirely fixable condition with the right medical equipment and knowledge, it often goes untreated in underdeveloped countries. Those women who suffer from it isolate themselves because they smell of urine. When the problem can be fixed, it's life saving for these women.

Medicine for Humanity was spearheaded by Dr. Leo Lagasse and Anne Lagasse with Dr. Gautam Chauduhri, Dr. Clifford Wheeless Jr., Dr. Jill Satorie, and Dr. Lisa Masterson. My brother helped them all to come into Eritrea, and they did an amazing job. I remember them working around the clock so they could treat as many women as possible and train Eritrean doctors on female maladies.

I was trying to convince myself that I could give up, but in the end, I knew I couldn't. Saleh's parting words to me said it all, "I know who you are. You're not a quitter. Obstacles are just another chapter. I know you're going to do something big, something that has never been done before." Saleh was not a man who gave encouragement easily—especially to family. His words were that much more powerful because of this, and they reverberated throughout my entire being.

For three days I marched around and around the city, trying to alleviate my sadness. Asmara is actually quite small and my walkabout was noticed. I started hearing about it, "You just keep walking. Are you ever going to stop?"

I didn't know how to answer my relatives, so I just continued to walk. But the more I circled the city, the more I realized that I was feeling like I had never left. Then it hit me. It was exactly like it was when I left.

When I was a kid, with the Ethiopian soldiers swarming the streets always looking for Freedom Fighters lurking in the shadows, there was a constant fear in people's eyes, a constant distrust in their stance towards each other. No one knew who was on what side. You always had to watch your conversation. You never knew if the person to whom you were talking was going to turn you in.

The post-independent Asmara was no different. People who were supposed to now be free weren't acting like it. The free press was abolished soon after Isaias took power, as I have noted, and more freedoms were soon stripped away. So the people in Asmara in 2006 had the same fear, the same distrust as the Eritrean people in the 1960s, 70s, and 80s. Every person was so monitored and controlled, even something as simple as playing cards was deemed illegal. Anything that made people feel free or heaven forbid *carefree* was strictly forbidden.

I would ask people in coffee shops a simple question and they would look at their companion as if to ask "whose side is she on?" They knew my brother worked for the "regime" (for that is really what it is. To call it the "government" does a huge disservice to that term.) But here's the truly frightening part—which side constituted the "good" side was totally up for grabs. You were either "good" or "bad," depending on how the other person viewed Isaias. Eritreans were not free. Far from it.

I walked away with enough sadness to realize that once again, I had to find a way to do something. I started poking around to see if I could actually help the refugees

Chapter 13 • The Astounding Truth

in the camps in the Sudan. I came up against every barrier imaginable. Official lines were closed. I couldn't even find anyone to tell me who I needed to contact. Sudan was still in the middle of its very public civil war. There was no way I would even be able to get a visa to travel into Sudan let alone find a way into the camps and see if there was something I could do through official channels.

I left Eritrea in 2006 broken hearted, but I was determined to find a way. That little girl who raced camels with the boys when she wasn't supposed to wasn't going to be defeated that easily.

I came home to Santa Monica. I searched for ways I could help the women and children from afar in the refugee camps. I may have been shut off from Eritrea, but Saleh was right. I could still help the people who were living in the refugee camps—generations of them at this point.

I founded my non-profit organization, Healing Bridges, in 2006, named for the bridges I wanted to help build for Eritreans so they could find their way to freedom.

CHAPTER 14

Trying to Find Bridges that Heal

By 2007, the egregious human rights atrocities in Eritrea were well-known. People were basically enslaved by the government in the National Service, working in inhumane conditions. Brothers and sisters were suspicious of each other because no one knew who was going to turn on whom. It was a massive culture of distrust.

But I had a plan. If I could give Eritrean women living in the camps something on which to pin even the tiniest hope—if not a way out—then it would be worth it.

I knew a trip to those camps would be dangerous. I knew it would require that I be ready so that when I got the "go ahead" sign, I wasn't held up. Robyn Quivers, a well-known radio personality, turned out to be my guardian angel. She really came out of nowhere and held a big fundraiser for Healing Bridges in New York to help. Before becoming a famous radio personality and actress, she was a trauma nurse. She knew, almost instinctively, what the women and children were experiencing, and told me that she needed to help.

I started talking to everyone who was willing to listen, and everyone I talked to connected to the idea of what I was creating.

By 2007, I also knew far more about the camps. There was, and is, over a half-million Eritrean refugees in the Sudan. The first refugee camps sprang up in eastern Sudan in 1967, not long after Selassie started his raids on my village. There have been attempts at repatriation over the years, and various places like Sweden will come in and select families to immigrate to their country. But the sad fact is very few of these refugees have been able to leave. Back in the late sixties, eighteen-hundred people crossed the border every month. As of 2017, there are an estimated five *thousand* people leaving every month.[4] In a country of around four million people, that is an enormous number, and these Eritreans make up most of the refugee population in Europe.

In recent years, the Eritrean government has concocted a strategy to keep the refugees out permanently. It has created instability in Eastern Sudan in order to manipulate a peace process whereby the Eritrean refugees would need to acquire Sudanese nationality and settle in Eastern Sudan.

Clearly Isaias has no intention of helping the refugees, and because they are still not yet permanently settled in the Sudan, the Eritreans in the camps suffer a continual, massive degradation.

The more I learned, the more I needed to find a way into those refugee camps.

---

[4] Matina Stevis and Joe Parkinson. *African Dictatorship Fuels Migrant Crisis: Thousands flee isolated Eritrea to escape life of conscription and poverty."* The Wall Street Journal. Updated Feb. 2, 2016. https://www.wsj.com/articles/eritreans-flee-conscription-and-poverty-adding-to-the-migrant-crisis-in-europe-1445391364

Chapter 14 • Trying to Find Bridges that Heal

I remembered the camps well from when I had fled Eritrea as a teenager. As I noted earlier, I never lived in them as I was able to stay with my Aunt Ne'rit in the nearby city of Kassala. But my Aunt would go visit people she knew in the camps, and I insisted that she take me with her. None of my cousins wanted anything to do with the camps. They were frightening and smelled horrendous. I felt such a heavy sadness in my heart when I went with her. I remember my aunt once saying to me, "You can't be this sad, it's not good for you." But I didn't know how *not* to be sad when I was a teenager, looking at that mass of humanity who had nothing.

Aunt Ne'rit would always insist that I understand something. She said as we would visit the camps, "Yes this is the camp, but we're all refugees." When I was young, I didn't think I was seeking "refuge" from anything. I was out of Eritrea. I was free! But I was as much a refugee as any other person who had to flee their country because of war.

Remembering that time still makes me shudder. Isaias is a power-hungry, despotic totalitarian dictator, in the same ilk as Stalin and Mao Tse-tung. They all profess to be "communist," even though I think they act beyond the boundaries of that ideology. However, "communism" I believe, is one of the reasons Eritrea suffers from a massive neglect of their basic human rights. No matter how much communism may be romanticized, the hard truth is, living under that kind of government destroys any sense of liberty. Now stop and think about that. Here in America we take the idea of freedom for granted. We talk about our freedoms all the time. But in a communist country, that is

Building the Impossible: A Refugee's Journey of Giving Back

a concept that is forbidden to talk about because if you did, the government feared, rightly so, that you would seek it out.

There is nothing romantic or good about living in a communist country. It is oppressive to the extreme. Looking back, that's why, even in horrendously appalling conditions, the refugees of my era (in 1978) generally had a look of hope. Everyone was so grateful to be free from the overwhelming oppression of the Ethiopian communists, who notably, were backed by the Soviet Union.

I wondered what the conditions were like in the camps now, after thirty years of neglect, abuse, and suppression beyond anything we could ever imagine here.

In late 2007, I still did not have any official way into the camps. But I had had enough. I was tired of hitting barrier after barrier. I decided to just start planning a trip. Somehow I would go directly to the camps, and there, I would find out from the refugees themselves exactly what they needed.

As I made my preparations, as always, many people stepped up to help. I decided that I wanted to take some high-school kids with me, at least for the first part of my journey. One of my original ideas was having a child in America sponsor a child in Eritrea. I thought that could still work.

Once I made the decision to go, I miraculously secured visas, not just for myself but for nine others, including three high-school students.

Finally, after six months of hard preparation and absolute determination, we arrived in the Sudan! It was late June, 2008. We flew into Khartoum, having travelled two days to get there. We then had to wait three days for approval to go to the refugee camp in Kassala. That is typical. The first trip

Chapter 14 • Trying to Find Bridges that Heal

is always hard in African countries where you are going to do work, especially with the refugees.

I knew I would need patience and dedication to see this project through, but even my patience was sorely tested. During those three days, we would be told to be ready to go to the camps, and then we would sit in the hotel lobby and wait…and wait…and nothing.

I used the time to interview people in Khartoum. I wanted to know how they came to be living in the city and what they did. I am always proud of my fellow Eritreans. They work hard and are willing to do most anything to survive. It's not easy to get jobs, but they would clean houses, drive buses, or do whatever menial labor they could. Some were going to college; some were trying to leave The Sudan.

Many of them told me that they'd never been to the refugee camp. I was surprised. "How is it you've never been to the refugee camp?" I asked one woman privately.

She wasn't apologetic about it. She told me, "First, it's impossible to get in, and I don't think I could take it. It would just break me. The people there are not really living; they're barely surviving day to day."

I told her that I had found a way to get into the camps and was only waiting for the final go-ahead. At that point, this woman looked at me intently and said, "I pray for you because I don't think you're going to be the same when you come out. I will continually pray that you emotionally survive it."

How do you respond to that. I didn't fully believe her. I couldn't imagine inside the camps were *that* bad.

After too many days of waiting, we finally got the papers approving our visit.

I don't think I can ever forget that car ride to the camps. The country we drove through was absolutely barren—the earth was cracked and utterly devoid of life. When we got to the camps, I immediately knew that woman in the city was not exaggerating. Whereas the refugees I had met when I went with my Aunt had hope, these people had none. They barely had enough water let alone food. The children had the tell-tale overextended bellies of the severely malnourished. The adults were shriveled, literally, from dehydration and lack of proper nutrition. There was absolutely no sanitation, so you can imagine the smell.

And that's when I saw the tents, the same old tents that were there when I came through in '78, but now shamefully dirty and torn. The people were equally as dilapidated and worn. Their eyes were dead. They could not leave the camps, they could do nothing but wait…and wait…and wait for what?

Suppression is the feeling that you can't fight back. These people were utterly disempowered, so devastated they no longer even thought about lifting a finger in their own defense. By all signs, Isaias had "won," and I knew I had taken a deep dive right into the middle of hell. The only thing I could do was hold my breath, physically, emotionally, and spiritually—and move on.

I knew what I had to do next. I had to talk to the mothers.

CHAPTER 15

You Want Me to Do What?

The group I brought stayed in the Sudan with me for ten days before they returned home to America. I was especially impressed with Lynn Rose's compassion and commitment to help. She was beautiful to watch, respectful of the Sudanese and their culture, and wonderfully courageous. She has also helped me continually since I returned to America and has been instrumental in making sure I made good on my promise to the mothers.

After I said good-bye to the group in Khartoum, I travelled back to Kassala. From there, I could more easily access the camps, and I was able to visit places the group couldn't. I used this to my advantage as best I could.

It wasn't easy. As I travelled farther into the interior of the camps, I had to be very mindful of what I was doing. I was pretty sure I was being watched. Isaias's informers were everywhere. But I decided I couldn't really think about it. The task at hand was too important and the feeling of utter despair too overwhelming. I pressed on.

Even now, these refugees don't know where their next meal is coming from. From the moment I walked into the camps, it felt heavy; the situation and the conditions were so bad. I quickly found they didn't know if they would have their basic necessities met on any given day. They certainly didn't have any real medical help, and they died of curable diseases frequently.

To make matters worse, the living conditions were horrendous. Pictures can't even really tell you how atrocious it really is. I was told that during a sandstorm, which is frequent, the old U.N. tents rip off their moorings. When the storm is over, the people go find their tents and put them back up. Obviously, they have no notion of anything permanent in their lives.

I kept thinking, "Oh my, they need clean water, they need food. They need some sort of sanitation system to stem the tide of disease. How do they live?"

The more I walked in the camps, the more I asked myself, how can a human being survive here? It was 120 degrees with no shelter. I didn't see a tree anywhere for miles. I felt paralyzed. This is when I learned that oftentimes the mothers wouldn't eat so that they would have food for their kids.

You could see the desperation and the discontent in the mothers' faces. In the fathers' faces, you could see the despair because they couldn't provide for their families.

It was almost impossible to get any information, so I finally decided to ask the mothers, point blank, what they wanted. To do that I had to find someone who was willing to talk to me as well as speak a language I could understand.

There was one woman I met, Lucia, who spoke very good English. I had actually met her with my group, and I found her again after the group left. I knew she would tell me what they *really* wanted. I still think she's one of the most remarkable women I have ever met.

So I asked her, "what do you want?

Chapter 15 • You Want Me to Do What?

She was very clear. "Mothers don't eat so that their children can go to school. It's very expensive. The families are required to buy all the school supplies—uniforms, textbooks, paper, pencils." And then without pausing, she stated emphatically, "We want a high school for our girls."

There it was. The request. It took everything I had to not blurt out, "you want *what*?"

To put her request into context: there are hundreds of U.N-supported refugee camps around the world. At that point, I don't believe a high school existed *in any of them*, not even for boys. This latter point is important because in this part of the world, it is a priority to educate the boys.

After I talked with Lucia, something really remarkable started happening. Maybe she spread the word, but no matter where I went, it was like they had had a meeting before I arrived. No matter which camp I visited, e*very* mother I talked to asked me if I could build a high school—not just any high school, but one for their girls.

I remember thinking, "These people have nothing—you would think they would ask me for something that is possible—water and food and shelter." Maybe that was my own bias because I knew it would be relatively easy to supply them with the necessities. But no, they were asking me for something that was absolutely impossible to achieve.

I never stayed in the camps overnight. I would return to Kassala for a few days and would spend my time asking various officials about the possibility of creating a school for the girls. Each time, after the person I talked to gave me a look that said, "keep dreaming," I would hear over and over, "There's not even one for the boys let alone the girls. Why would you want to build one for girls?

They couldn't really understand why I was putting the girls first. They thought it would be far more appropriate to ask about a school for the boys.

This prompted me to ask the mothers, "If there's no high school for anyone, why do you ask for one for your girls? Why do you think that's possible for me to achieve?

They said, "We know it's impossible, but you're here, and you're asking what we need, so that's what we're telling you." They would then say, "It might take you five years or even ten but that doesn't matter. We've been here for forty—ten more won't matter."

Those who tried and failed probably did so because a project like this takes a very very long time, so they would give up. I knew what I was up against. It would not only take time and money to get something like a high school for girls built, but I also knew it would be emotionally taxing because of all the bureaucracy and prejudice I would have to overcome.

But my mission was now clear. I would have to let go of the idea of starting a Grameen bank for the short term. I decided then and there that I was going to build that high school for girls no matter what.

I said to the mothers I continued to meet, "I know it's impossible to do this, but I'll do everything in my power to ensure your girls will have a high school."

I could see that school, filled with girls, helping them find their way in life. I envisioned some spark of life in their eyes where there was none previously. It was an image I carried with me always, for it gave me the strength to endure what was to come.

Chapter 15 • You Want Me to Do What?

It is remarkable how utterly willing those mothers were to put their faith in me. As I would tell them of my resolve, I could see, ever so slightly, a flicker of something in their face—hope maybe? Whatever it was, it signified life. They gave me their blessing, and I was grateful for it. I knew I would need all the help I could get to make their wish a reality.

CHAPTER 16

Victory ... Or Defeat?

I had my marching orders, but I still held my breath. I had no expertise in this area nor did I know who to ask. I thought maybe, if someone built a school anywhere in the vicinity, I could ask this or that organization how they had done it. At least it gave me a starting point.

I was still in the Sudan, and I knew that I had to make the best use of my time. I knew I first had to find a local organization who could physically build the school. But I also knew that would be very difficult. With the embargo to the Sudan, there were not a lot of non-governmental organizations (NGOs) I could choose from. If you want to build a school in India, for example, you just raise the funds, put it in the bank, and the local organization implements the work. But in Sudan, I couldn't do that. I had to go through all the proper bureaucratic channels.

I spent the remaining part of my trip meeting with local organizations and searching for the various leaders who were in positions to help. Sometimes it was impossible to meet them. I would wait for hours, even days, to be introduced, and…then…nothing. There was one person whom I knew could help, and I waited every day for a week to meet him. One day I waited eight hours and twenty minutes. He was that important. I finally met him, and he told me that he had purposefully kept me waiting, hoping I would give up. It only took him a few minutes to tell me what I needed to do to make the high school a reality. It still all seemed impossible, but at least now I could form a plan.

I also met with all kinds of local organizations that could actually do the construction, but I was stopped at every turn. No organization that I met with was licensed to work with an American company or non-profit because of the embargo. I found out who the sanctioned organizations were from the state department—including the U.N. But they all charged a percentage of the donations—from 18 percent to 25 percent—just for their overhead. So if it would cost $100,000 to build a school, the U.N. for example, would require that I raise $125,000, and they take the $25,000 off the top. I was in shock, but I didn't have time to get angry. I needed to move on.

I left the Sudan with no organization lined up. I had an impossible task to achieve, and even if the government cleared my request, I still didn't know how I would get the funds there.

It all seemed pretty overwhelming.

I spent two days on airplanes and in airports wondering how in the world I was going to accomplish this task. I was also having a *very* difficult time breathing, something that I had noticed right before I left the Sudan.

On the way back to America, I still felt like I was holding my breath, both literally and figuratively. I had promised those mothers in the camps that I would get their high school built, but the very people who were supposed to be

Chapter 16 • Victory ... Or Defeat?

helping them, and by extension me, didn't seem like they really cared.

I felt myself sinking deeper and deeper into something I couldn't name. I'll never forget the second I walked through the door of my apartment, something inside me crumbled. While I was in the Sudan, I couldn't get emotional. I couldn't show weakness or fear. While I was in the camps, I was aware of a gnawing sense of pain everywhere in my body, but I didn't pay any attention to it because I didn't have time.

I deteriorated quickly. I only told a couple of people that I was back. I didn't want to relive what I had just experienced until I was emotionally able to answer questions without breaking down. I felt an enormous and overwhelming sadness and grief. But I couldn't cry. I couldn't do anything. I didn't think I was sick, but I do know that I felt myself plunging into an emotional darkness, something I had never experienced before. That and the pain in my chest and lungs grew worse.

As I fell deeper into a depression, my health was failing, and I became overwhelmed. I was given a task, and it looked like I was going to fail. I couldn't get the faces of all the mothers out of my mind. I couldn't bear the thought of telling them that I wasn't able to provide the one thing that they wanted most—an education for their daughters.

A couple of days later, I ended up in the ICU. I had a breathing capacity of 30–35 percent. In other words, I wasn't able to breathe on my own, at all. I fell into a coma and people feared for my life.

When I was finally released from the hospital, I couldn't even walk a block without my chest tightening and feeling like I was going to faint.

Everything felt so surreal. Before I left for the Sudan, I was in excellent shape. I was training for a triathlon. Now I could barely walk a block.

I took a hard look at the situation. I remembered what I had lived through before, and in that I found the courage to move forward. I couldn't run from the soldiers this time, but I could email. I could sit and talk on the phone. Well sort of. At first I would cough after every other word. But I could do *something*.

It was like I had been smoking heavily my entire life. But with my oxygen tank by my side, I was forced to sit and call the Sudan and connect with whomever I could. I would sleep during the day so I could be up all night while that part of the world was awake. Even though my doctors told me to rest, I didn't listen. I knew I could survive anything.

The first six months I spent hours on the phone talking to endless amounts of people. Friends of friends, people who knew people who knew people, someone who then connected me with someone else who would then connect me to yet another person.

I wasn't going to give up. My life had been spared, and that was my sign, I was determined to keep going. I kept telling everyone I contacted. "I want to build a high school in the refugee camp."

Everyone I talked to said, "There's no high school in the refugee camp."

I said, "I know, I want to build one." Finally, I got word that I would be allowed to build a high school. I knew what that meant. They didn't get it. They only said, "high school," not "high school for girls."

Back to the phones.

Chapter 16 • Victory ... Or Defeat?

Everyone I talked to said, again, "that's impossible." I didn't listen.

I kept calling.

"What? A high school for girls? Why?" Was the common response. I realized I had to make it about the boys. I knew that to the officials, you educate a boy because he's the one who is supposed to get a job.

My answer became a mantra, "Well, if we educate the girls," I would say to my incredulous listener, "then they will become an educated mother who can then help educate her son better. She can help him with his homework, help make him a better man."

Their response was unanimous, "Oh, I've never thought about it that way."

It took another six months to get permission, but I finally succeeded. I made phone calls to various people, some every day or every-other day, some every week. And piece by piece it happened. I got the okay to build the high school *for girls*. Then I was told that there would be land provided on which to build the high school, even though it would only be "temporary."

I said, "fine." The refugees had been there "temporarily" for forty years. It didn't matter. I had what I needed: permission and land.

While I was working on getting all the right permissions, I was also looking for an organization that had the right state department clearance to which I could transfer the funds. I called any organization that had a clearance to work in the Sudan. I called and called. I finally found one after about a year, called ARAHA—the American Relief Agency for the Horn of Africa. The CEO had contacted me before I went to the Sudan and we had talked a little bit about how they worked in the Sudan, Ethiopia, and Somalia.

I didn't contact him right away when I returned because I was jaded. I didn't think his organization would be licensed to work in the Sudan. When I did finally contact him and asked him again if he had a right to work in Sudan, he said yes.

I asked him straight up "What's your fee?"

He said, "What do you mean."

I asked, "What's your fee."

He said, "We charge 5 percent."

Sold.

We became partners. We agreed that I would fund the high school for girls, and ARAHA would do the work. It's been a perfect marriage ever since.

It was now a little over a year since I had left the Sudan. I had practically died when I fell into a coma when I returned because I was so distraught over the idea of not being able to keep my promise.

But it was going to happen! The high school for girls in the Eritrean refugee camp was going to get built! I relished the idea of calling Lucia to tell her that her daughters and all the daughters of all the mothers I met had their wish.

When I did call, it was one of the happiest and best phone calls of my entire life!

I still had to raise some more funds. I had kept Robyn Quivers' donations safe, and that provided a large chunk of what I needed. I was selling tee shirts to friends and friends of friends. I was still slowly recovering, and so I didn't have the energy to do what I used to, hustle all around the country, talking to people for hours every day.

Chapter 16 • Victory ... Or Defeat?

Work started on the school in September, 2009. We put in six classrooms, two offices, three bathrooms, a library, a sort of makeshift kitchen so the girls could have one meal a day. This in itself is unheard of. The building itself is in the middle of nowhere. I wanted it situated between three camps so girls from each camp could attend.

The school took seven months to build. To get anything that size built in Africa in that time frame is unheard of—and not just in the refugee camps but pretty much throughout the continent. For ARAHA to get the materials, bricks and cement, the wood and whatever else was needed—and to have it done in less than a year—was a miracle!

The school opened in 2010 by sheer intention. There were so many obstacles to overcome—so much bureaucracy, so many misunderstandings—but in the end, I thank all those people who could have stopped me but didn't. They saw the wisdom of helping the girls become educated. For those girls become the women who bear the future children of Eritrea. As Dr. Leo Lagasse, who runs Medicine for Humanity, once said, "If women can't be healthy, the country can't prosper." Women's health and education go hand-in-hand. When the women are educated, a country is far more able to flourish.

Unfortunately, while this was a monumental reason to celebrate, my heart was heavy with loss and my health was continuing to decline. In 2009 my father passed away. It was the first time I lost someone so close, so special to me. My father was my rock. He had instilled in me not just the idea of freedom and independence but the importance of service to others. Through him, I had a well of support, love, and strength from which I could always draw. His love has never left me, but I have felt the absence of his presence keenly.

But I didn't just lose my father that year. A few months after my father passed, I got the news. Saleh was dead.

CHAPTER 17

The Leader and the Minister of Eritrea

Officially, the cause of Saleh's death is listed as "heart attack."

I shouldn't have been shocked by what happened. We all knew what was coming. He reiterated to me the last time I saw him, "I'm not going to last that long, but I'm going to continue serving the Eritrean people."

Still, the loss was devastating to my family and to the Eritrean people. But I knew my brother's interests at heart, even to the end. And the people of Eritrea knew as well. Hundreds of people attended his funeral, and it stands as a last testament to what he tried to accomplish.

My brother came to America in 1972, but by 1978 he was back in Eritrea, finding a way to help the Freedom Fighters. He made it his mission to support the Freedom Fighters financially and let the world know what they had done. To accomplish this mission, he appeared on TV in Minnesota throughout the 1970s.

By the time of Eritrean Independence, he left his job as a health professional and moved back to Eritrea. He became the Minister of the Marine in 1993 and in 1997 was named the Minister of Health. He had high hopes for Eritrea and what Isaias was going to do for the country.

By 2001, Saleh knew the truth. In the 1990s, he believed Isaias would lead the country to prosperity, but as the years went by, it became clear that the revolutionary leader only knew how to lead revolutions, not a peaceful government.

As a revolutionary leader of the EPLF and as the leader of Eritrea, Isaias demanded absolute, unquestioning allegiance. When he became "president," all his ministers knew if they didn't support their "supreme commander," they were dead men. They would drink themselves to death, or they would become so sick they would die of heart attacks. Or they would sometimes just mysteriously disappear.

Shortly before Saleh's death, Isaias sent him to Massawa. This is one of the dictator's tactics. To demoralize those opposed to him, he ships them from one place to another. It always works. The ministers end up dead.

When Isaias sent Saleh to Massawa, he also transferred Saleh's position from Minister of Health back to Minister of Marine. At that time, Saleh knew his time had come.

Saleh went to Massawa as ordered. But he was heartbroken.

The day that he died, he had lunch with Isaias, and shortly after that, it was reported that he had foam coming out of his mouth.

Eritreans around the country were devastated. They loved Saleh, and I can understand why. He worked hard for them and he had their best interests at heart. And that was his downfall. Even now, in Isaias's mind, no one can be more admired than Isaias. No Eritrean should be more loyal to anyone but the grand ruler.

Chapter 17 • The Leader and the Minister of Eritrea

However, Saleh's loyalty to the Eritrean people is what we will all remember, and I know I'm not the only one who is grateful for all that he did for Eritrea.

A Tribute to My Brother

What my brother, Saleh, accomplished in Eritrea, is, in a word, remarkable. No one will ever know the extent or the amount of duress he was under as he worked to better the health care system in Eritrea. But that he accomplished many great things is a matter of known record.

While time moves ever forward, his death still haunts me. Maybe if I take a moment to honor him and what he did for the Eritrean people, I can find a way to let him rest in peace in my heart.

Saleh's strategy with the people was brilliant. He created mobile clinics to go from village to village, assigning nurses to teach the villagers how to take care of themselves and how to minimize the spread of germs. He would often go himself with these mobile clinics, especially to the lowlands. Everywhere he went he was accepted. He was very approachable. He was always kind and compassionate. He would sit on the floor and talk to the people in their own language.

Saleh worked with many western and Eritrean doctors, but one of his dear friends, Dr. Haile Mezghebe, worked extensively with Saleh to bring medical missions to Eritrea through an organization called Physicians for Peace with Huda Ayas, Ph.D. and Dr. Ellie Hamburger. Saleh was also instrumental in bringing many other organizations into the country, such as Medicine for Humanity, which I've already noted.

Later, Dr. Mezghebe helped to create the connection between the George Washington University Medical Center where he was a fellow and the Eritrean Ministry of Health to create the Orotta School of Medicine, the first medical school in Eritrea.

Dr. Mezehebe has kept all his correspondence with Saleh, as they worked to create better healthcare in a country torn by war and increasingly oppressed by Isaias. It shows the great love and care these men had for each other and the country of their birth, Eritrea.

So that you can understand how important Saleh is to the Eritrean people and to my story, I am taking a moment to excerpt some of that correspondence, as well as other writing Dr. Mezghebe has done about my brother.

To understand their background, Dr. Mezghebe writes:

> *My connection to Saleh goes back to the 1970's when we were both active in the pro-EPLF student movement in North America. We knew each other through the movement but I was not in his close circle of friends. Our friendship started in earnest after Saleh returned to Eritrea and became Minister of Fisheries. When he became Minister of Health, our friendship flourished and Saleh became a major influence on my personal and professional life over the subsequent ten to fourteen years.*

The quest to improve healthcare in Eritrea started with independence. In an official letter from the Ministry of Health dated January 18, 2000, Saleh writes Dr. Mezghebe requesting trained Radiologists who could provide training and services at a then newly opened "polyclinic" that

Chapter 17 • The Leader and the Minister of Eritrea

offered CT Scans and MRIs—something that had been missing from Eritrea.

Dr. Mezghbebe summed up Saleh very well when he wrote of the early years of independence. At that time, the Eritrean government was still able to develop the country, and one of their tactics was reaching out to "Diaspora Eritreans," people who had left during the war and had made a life elsewhere but still wanted to find a way to help their homeland.

> *During the early years of independence, the leadership as a whole was receptive to the idea of partnership with Diaspora Eritreans, in particular, but other entities in general. I believe Saleh had a robust and solid understanding of what these potential partnerships meant and how to go about establishing them to the betterment of the people and country of Eritrea. He was a master at quick analysis of any issue and then making solid decisions for or against an idea. Once he committed himself, he was like a pit bull; he would not let go before its completion.*

However, these partnerships were fraught with distrust from the beginning. In an email dated June 18, 2002, Saleh wrote Dr. Mezghebe an email that is as telling as much for what it says as for what it doesn't:

> "Dear. Dr. Haile:
>
> I just received your email note.
>
> "I am afraid I failed to assure you in my last letter that I meant not to reproach you nor blame any one in particular for what was written.

My intention was and is for us all to identify the organizational and structural problems in our health care delivery system, so as to find a common solution in the interest of our people. That and that only matters, the rest is irrelevant.

"Thanks for the kind words in your note. My contributions, as it were, are very limited. I believe, if those who wish Eritrea and its people well, are given a chance to contribute in its health care development—in these difficult times—then together we will meet the considerable challenges we face quite successfully. No doubt you are a dependable ally in that national task; your efforts are impressive.

Finally, as we are engaged in a monumental task for national reconstruction, there will be those who would have us do less, criticize to immobilize, blinded by hate and jealousy—they refuse to see the difference between self-interest and common good. They are few but deadly; one need to be aware of this without exaggerating their effort too much.

It is worthwhile to remember that the majority, who respect the good deeds, admire the vision, selflessly support the mission and the work we all do with enthusiasm. Our task is to tell the difference with care."

The Ministry of Health was considered highly dysfunctional, even "in shambles" as Dr. Mezghebe described, as Eritrea gained its independence. Both the regional hospitals

Chapter 17 • The Leader and the Minister of Eritrea

as well as the major hospital in Asmara were in very bad disrepair with virtually no medicine or other essential supplies.

There was, of course, enormous pressure to conform to whatever Isaias wanted. But Saleh forged ahead, always keeping his heart and mind focused on the goal. He didn't want his people to suffer needlessly. He wanted to update the Health Care system and bring medicine into Eritrea, and while he was alive, he made great strides.

Dr. Mezghebe writes:

> *...The country saw its greatest level of improvement in the infrastructure and delivery of the health care system when the late Saleh Meky became the Minister of Health (about 1996). He used his incredible visionary mind to establish relationships with non-governmental and governmental agencies to lobby for funding and support from outside the country.*

Eventually, the Ministry of Health became the showcase ministry for the entire country. Saleh oversaw the construction of a modern two-hundred bed hospital in Mendefera and another one at Barentu and at Gindae. Not only were these hospitals modern but also well equipped.

Dr. Mezghebe tells of Saleh's other accomplishments with pride:

- Saleh single handedly established a first-ever blood bank center which won multiple awards and recognitions by the International Red Cross as a center of Excellence.
- He championed the eradication of malaria. Eritrea became the first African country to do so.

- Under Saleh's leadership, maternal and infant mortality dropped by half, and the rate of vaccination more than doubled.

Saleh was able to use his position in the government to oversee the process of applying for and administrating a World Bank loan. Dr. Mezghebe tells the story of what happened:

Though I do not have detailed knowledge of the specific agreements between the State of Eritrea and the World Bank, I do know that once the World Bank loan was approved for health-related developments, Saleh committed his life to making it work for the people of Eritrea. It is clear that he could not have done what he did without the approval and blessing of the President. However, once given the go ahead, Saleh used his intellect, vision and drive to implement, supervise and deliver the construction of the modern hospitals (noted above).

That Saleh and Dr. Mezghebe continually encountered major obstacles throughout their decade of working together is certain. One email exchange was particularly poignant. Dr. Mezghebe wrote Saleh:

"I must tell you that any time we read about yet another NGO being kicked out of Eritrea or a foreigner being asked to leave or movement of visitors being restricted, it makes people here very nervous. The US Ambassador has already warned our delegation (when we visited his office in Asmara) how difficult it is to work with the Eritrean government; how it (Eritrea) can

Chapter 17 • The Leader and the Minister of Eritrea

suddenly reverse its policy and terminate any agreement without any explanation whatsoever.

Saleh, without changing the core value of the government's policy, is there anything we can do to help reverse this image that seems to haunt us. Must we kick everyone out? And do we need to do it in the way we do it? Our harsh methods lack diplomatic tact and they leave us open for criticisms. I must tell you, it is becoming increasingly difficult to agitate and work on behalf of Eritrea.

Dr. Mezghebe and Saleh soldiered on, and as Dr. Mezghebe said of him:

It is fair to say that the successful modernization of the healthcare infrastructure and the institutions for the teaching of healthcare providers in Eritrea were in large part due to the relentless effort and vision of Minister Saleh Meky.

After Saleh's death, the medical missions that Saleh played a major role in bringing to Eritrea through Physicians for Peace all but ended. However, the Orotta Medical School did open, and the best tribute I can pay to my brother is to reprint the dedication of the first graduating class of Orotta, for it captures the essence of my brother:

On this momentous occasion of celebrating the first ever graduation of highly qualified "in-country trained surgeons," it is only fitting that we pay tribute to the contribution of our former Minister of Health, Mr. Saleh Meky.

Building the Impossible: A Refugee's Journey of Giving Back

It is a matter of record that Minister Saleh played a key role in starting the Orotta School of Medicine and the Post Graduate Medical Education Program. His accomplishments are many, but it is obvious that Minister Saleh could not have done what he did had it not been for the solid support of the top leadership of the country and many dedicated staff within the ministry.

However, there is no denying that at the end of the day, it was he who brought every thing together to a point of maturation and delivery. For this and many other accomplishments, his legacy will endure.

Saleh as a man of great intellect, competence, vision, high principles, a sense of fun and truly buoyant personality. In his daily work and commitment to the people of Eritrea, he was a man of uncompromising integrity and devotion with a remarkable sense of purpose. In all his endeavors, Saleh was not afraid to display anger or frustration when appropriate. However, he never allowed cynicism to dull his ever present enthusiasm and hope for the future. His enthusiasm and commitment remained forever fresh and vibrant.

As a leader, he ably showed us the way, gave us direction and he acted and took ownership of events rather than just react to them. He showed his courage by promoting and defending views and projects that were bold, new, and visionary but not necessarily popular at the time.

Chapter 17 • The Leader and the Minister of Eritrea

One of his great attributes was how readily he acknowledged the contribution of others. He took great pleasure from the success and achievements of others. He was the ultimate selfless and self-sacrificing leader. Even his death is a testimony to this fact in that he feared he would not abandon the people of Eritrea for too long if he were to take time off to attend to his personal health.

Until the time of his untimely death, his love and affection for the students, staff of the Ministry of Health, and indeed for the people of Eritrea remained robust and all encompassing.

When we think of Saleh, we shall remember his intense commitment to the people of Eritrea, his superb leadership, sense of confidence, his genuine concern for his fellowmen, his great and bold sense of humor, his tenacity for the principles that he believed in, his relentless energy, his creative imagination and his friendship. For all that he had done on behalf of so many, we say THANK YOU and we promise to work diligently to continue the legacy of hard work and dedication that you left behind.

May you rest in peace and rise in glory.

While Saleh is gone, my wish is that his work will continue on in the country and in the camps. My great hope is the Eritrean refugees will somehow realize the dream we both shared for Eritrea: that it will once again stand proud, independent, with a government that willingly follows the rule of law and where human rights—which include the right to good health, education, and freedom of movement—are honored and protected.

CHAPTER 18

The School

It is a testament to what we as human beings can accomplish if we want something done. By the time construction started on the Shagarab high school for girls, there was so much intention behind it, it had no choice but to get done.

Everyone I talked to, no matter from what country in Africa, kept telling me how unusual it was to get something like that done so quickly "It takes about a year and a half with local workers," I was told over and over.

All I can say is that we were really blessed to have found ARAHA. They helped me build that school and have kept it going since.

I am also proud to say that the school HealingBridges helped build accommodates over a hundred and fifty girls at one time. It educates ninth through twelfth grades, and it is built, as I wished, in the middle of Shagarab, so that girls could attend from the three surrounding camps. It opened in July of 2010.

While it was being built, Lucia, the mother who was so outspoken about getting the high school, would call me, thrilled. She would give me progress reports. She would go every few days and see the cement and brick going up.

No one could quite believe that an actual high school was being built up there, in those camps; and it was even more unbelievable that this was going to be for the *girls*. They had never seen anything like it before in the camps. The construction was being done with real cement—the mortar, the bricks, everything. The refugees knew it would last, unlike the bricks they made with hay and mud.

Lucia would pass the messages from the other mothers and the girls. "It's becoming a reality." Their gratitude was unbounded, and they left me speechless.

The mothers, my sisters, are so proud their girls are attending high school. They tell me how excited they were the day their daughters received their backpacks, school supplies, uniforms, and shoes. While the school was being built, I turned my attention to getting donations for the students so that their parents didn't have to pay for anything. It's an ongoing project—something like this isn't funded just once but required constant attention. Basic supplies as well as clothing come at a cost in the Sudan, especially in the camps, so it takes constant diligence to continue the flow of funds.

I still feel the weight of suppression on all those still living in Eritrea, but with the school, I found not just hope but the knowledge that we can create anything we want to when we put our minds, hearts, and souls into the project. I knew that I was giving something so much more important to those mothers and their daughters than food and drink. I was giving them something far more valuable—a way for them to provide for themselves. That is the greatest gift anyone can ever give to anyone else.

Chapter 18 • The School

When I got word that the school was finished, I thought, "Wow, this is just the beginning. I have this responsibility for all those girls." I really feel like the girls in that school are my children, and so like any good mother, I must make sure they're provided for. The work is worth it.

I love hearing that this school has evolved. The girls go to school in the mornings, and we've opened it up for the boys in the afternoons. I am pleased to report that the graduating class of 2017 is seventy girls and boys, the highest ever in the school.

But I never lose sight of its original purpose. The whole point of a high school for girls is to give these young women a way to break the cycle of poverty by teaching them how to be self-sustaining. What we don't really understand here is that, in Africa, and especially in the refugee camps, once you finish high school, you're practically in a different society. High school graduates can easily get a job. For the refugees, that means a way out of the camps.

The Executive Director of ARAHA said it best in an open letter he sent in early 2017:

In addition to teaching hundreds of school-aged children, the school provides employment for more than fifteen adult refugees in the camp, who teach, cook, guard, and provide nursing services.

The positive impact of the Shegerab Secondary School has been profound. Girls who had no expectation of receiving an education beyond the elementary level are now in college. The boys, too, have had more success than ever due to their education, which has opened up work opportunities that would otherwise have been unavailable to them.

The positive impact has been felt not just by students, but by everyone. Increased access to higher education has had positive social and health impacts throughout the camp. For example, prior to the establishment of the school, girls in the camp had no opportunities once they finished elementary school, so their parents pushed them to marry at very young ages. These girls, already malnourished, were struggling with health complications during pregnancy and labor, leading to many cases of premature birth and maternal death in the camp.

Opening the school offered these girls more time to mature and delay marriage until a more ideal age. In the first year the school opened, many girls approached ARAHA's representatives to thank them for the educational opportunities that were now open to them, and for preventing the early marriages they'd witnessed other girls near their ages go through. Now, when these girls graduate with more extensive education, they will positively influence their own children, continuing an upward cycle potentially for generations to come.

Education breaks the cycle of poverty. Education opens the doors of possibility. We are in the process of funding a school for the boys in the camps. This is most pressing; there is growing concern because girls and boys shouldn't be in the same building, so we need to get this next school

Chapter 18 • The School

built quickly so that this wonderful opportunity for everyone can continue.

When the boy's school is done, I dream of putting schools in each of the Eritrean refugee camps in Sudan.

I will still work to put a Grameen bank into those places that would benefit from it. I hope also one day to continue to do my work in Eritrea. But no matter what else happens, what I do know is that while there is breath, wonderful life-giving breath in my body, I know that there will be a school in those camps to give the kind of lasting hope to the people I always wanted to help the most.

The school for those girls has become a true beacon of hope to all the women in those camps. It is a testament to the tenacity of the human spirit. It will remain my proudest accomplishment.

I have faced death many times in my life, but I don't think I was truly living until I had accomplished that dream. Now, our job is to band together to ensure it continues.

Epilogue

I grew up watching the women in my village weaving baskets with patterns created only in their minds. I watched them create amazing works of usable art with their hands—not just the baskets in which we could store large amounts of food but the clothing we wore on our backs and an amazing array of everything we needed for our homes.

I grew up believing that I could do what I set out to accomplish. My story is the potential story of hundreds of others in my beloved Eritrea and her refugees. And I believe my story is positively mundane compared to the other heroic feats of bravery of Eritrean men and women who save themselves every day from the brutal hands of the dictator, Isaias.

I cherish every story I hear, and I am heartened because many are telling stories of what's happened to them and others in Eritrea. But many more are fearful to speak out because they feel like if they do, their family will be punished. By telling my story, I hope I give courage to others to tell theirs, for only when the world is overwhelmed by the atrocities that are happening daily, even as I write this, will the people of the world be able to stand up and speak out collectively against the injustice in Eritrea.

Here in America, we take the idea of "liberty" and "security," for granted. We know it is our right, and we demand it. But for the people living in Eritrea and in the camps, those fundamental tenets of our very existence are considered privileges for only a chosen few—and for those who have any semblance of "security," I wonder what they have compromised to buy that uneasy peace.

So I will continue to speak up, to tell of the horrendous violations of basic human rights. the murders, the lack of freedom that is an everyday reality for too many in this world. But more importantly, I also want to make sure that by speaking up, I can inspire women who think that they may have lost their voice—or feel like they never had it—because they know that someone, somewhere on this great earth, is fighting for them. If that gives them strength to stand up and find the courage to not just survive, but find a way to live a better life, then my time on this earth will not have been in vain.

I proudly carry the Eritrean ability to create beautiful things in the face of extraordinary hardship—whether that be the shirt on my back or the buildings that carry forward generations of intelligent, capable women into a better world.

I called my nonprofit Healing Bridges because back in 2006, when I was going through the process of creating my organization, I knew that the only way to help Eritrea survive was to find ways to build bridges over the truly gruesome destruction they live with every minute of their lives. Eritrean courage and tenacity are truly the hidden treasures that have become the foundation of Healing Bridges, and I want to foster that in every girl throughout the world.

• Epilogue

Help, real help, is possible. I see it happen daily.

There is an enormous amount of work that still needs to be done for Eritrea. The people are not free. They are deprived of their basic human rights daily by a government who only wants to control them—mind, body, and spirit. Eritrea's only material asset is its long coast line. It doesn't have diamonds or oil. But it has a people who could once again be indomitable. They fought for their freedom for thirty years. That spirit still lives in them. I know it does. We just have to find real ways to help them discover it again.

They are a proud, hard-working people, Eritreans. We need to help them continue to fight for their freedom. My hope is that you will join me, and together we can work towards creating a healing bridge of freedom and peace, first from America to Eritrea and then expand that movement throughout the world.

Afterword

To capture the essence of a human being—that is the purpose and the power of stories, and that is exactly what Zebiba Shekhia has captured in this book, *Building the Impossible: A Refugee's Journey of Giving Back*. Here is a story of how one woman escaped, not just the horrors of war and genocide, but something that is more insidious, more destructive even, than murder—poverty. But, it is precisely because she has escaped that hellish fate that she feels that she must go back and help the women and children in all the war-torn areas of Africa.

Everyday human beings are not one-dimensional entities; they are excitingly multi-dimensional and indeed very colorful, and it is this multi-dimensionality that we must not only celebrate but allow to develop if we are going to solve poverty and all that comes with it. Zebiba's organization, Healing Bridges, is one that "got it." Helping the women and children marries education with economic self-sufficiency, and that is key. We most certainly must help to educate the poor, but that is only part of the battle. If we don't put a viable economic system into place that can support more highly educated people, then we've created another problem—educated people but no jobs.

I have long contended that it is definitely not the lack of skills which make poor people poor. Poverty is not created by the poor; it is created by the institutions and policies which surround them. And in order to help institutions reform and effect the appropriate policy changes, it is vital that we recognize that the poor have skills which, as of now, remain unutilized or under-utilized. Zebiba talks about this in her book when she tells the story of her mother being able to weave beautiful baskets, but when she was a young woman, divorced, with no-where to turn, she couldn't convert that skill into a money-making venture. With a Grameen loan, she could have, and so could her fellow countrywomen who have equally valuable skills.

Grameen created a methodology and an institution around the financial needs of the poor, and created access to credit on reasonable terms enabling the poor to build on their existing skills to earn a better income in each cycle of loans that they take from the Grameen bank. For those of you who are unfamiliar with Grameen Bank and Grameencredit, its principle feature is reaching the poor.

It is a non-negotiable mission, and to achieve it, Grameencredit gives high priority on building social capital/social entrepreneurship, where people are willing to give their time and their money to help build a world that is free from poverty. It gives special emphasis on the formation of human capital and concern for protecting the environment. It monitors children's education, provides scholarships and student loans for higher education. For the formation of human capital, it makes efforts to bring technology, like mobile phones and solar power, to the poor across the

• Afterword

world, and it promotes manual power being replaced by mechanical power.

What makes Zebiba and Healing Bridges so compelling as both an individual and an organization is that she believes that charity is not an answer to poverty. Charity only helps poverty to continue. It creates dependency and takes away the individual's initiative to break through the wall of poverty. That dependency, in turn, helps keep the world in turmoil. Unleashing of energy and creativity in each human being is the answer to poverty, and, as Zebiba so compellingly argues, it can also start the process of creating "the healing bridges of peace," that she calls for at the end of this wonderful book.

Peace, real lasting peace, comes when people are free to choose their own direction in life. There is so much untapped potential in our world, and if we can give a hand-up to those who are suffering, if we continue to seek to help each other become better human beings able to create our own paths, then Zebiba's mission and my mission will be complete.

Dr. Muhammad Yunus
2006 Nobel Peace Prize Winner
For more information about Professor Yunus and his work, please visit
www.yunuscentre.org

To find out how you can help Zebiba do her work with Healing Bridges, please visit www.buildingtheimpossible.com. Profits from this book, as well as other products developed for Healing Bridges, go to support the work Zebiba does. Thank you for your interest and your help.

About the Author

Zebiba Shekhia fled Eritrea in 1978 to escape the atrocities being committed by the Ethiopian totalitarian dictator, Mengistu. Travelling through the Sudan, Middle East, Europe, and landing, finally, in America, Zebiba always vowed to find a way to go back and help the women and children left behind.

She spent years trying to work with the Eritrean government in the areas of education and micro financing; however, the government denied her requests to help at every turn. Finally Saleh Meky, the Eritrean Minister of Health (her brother), told her, "You have tried your very best, but if you continue, you're going to get in a lot of trouble, and there will be no way for me to help you. Go to the Eritrean refugee camp in Eastern Sudan. Help them. Don't come back here."

In 2006, Zebiba founded Healing Bridges, an organization dedicated to helping Eritrean children get the education they need—and deserve. Healing Bridges helped various schools in Kassala, Sudan, and with ARAHA (the American Relief Agency for the Horn of Africa), built a high school for girls in the refugee camps in Shegerab, Sudan, at the request of the mothers. It was the first high school for girls to ever be built in the refugee camps.

Zebiba continues to help in the refugee camps. She lives in Los Angeles. Please visit www.BuildingtheImpossible.com.

References

For more information about the school and the plight of Eritreans currently, please visit:
www.araha.org
www.asmarino.com
www.neweriuk.org
www.eritreadigest.com
www.hrc-Eritrea.org
www.awate.com

For a more in-depth look at Eritrean history and the recent human rights abuses in Eritrea, please read:

Sadia Hassanen. *Repatriation, Integration, or Resettlement: The Dilemmas of Migration among Eritrean Refugees in Eastern Sudan* (Red Sea Press, 2017).

Thomas Keneally. To Asmara: A Novel of Africa. Thomas Keneally. Grand Central Publishing (Reprint, 1990).

Abeba Tesfagiorgis. *A Painful Season and A Stubborn Hope: The Odessey of an Eritrean Mother.* (Red Sea Press, 1992).

Martin Plaut. *Understanding Eritrea: Inside Africa's Most Repressive State.* (Oxford University Press, 2017.)

Michela Wrong. *I Didn't Do It for You: How the World Betrayed a Small African Nation.* (Harper Perennial. 2006).

Dan Connell. *Against All Odds: A Chronicle of the Eritrean Revolution with a New Afterword on the Postwar Transition.* (Red Sea Press, 1997).

Salem Solomon and Tewelde Tesfagabir. "Eritrea Closes Hundreds of Businesses for Bypassing Banks. VOANews. https://www.voanews.com/a/eritrea-businesses-closed-by-passing-banks/4196755.html. January 7, 2018.

Report of the Commission of Inquiry on human rights in Eritrea. United Nations Human Rights Council. June 8, 2016. http://www.ohchr.org/EN/HRBodies/HRC/CoIEritrea/Pages/commissioninquiryonhrinEritrea.aspx

"ERITREA: Canadian Appeal Court Affirms Eritreans' Slavery and Forced Labour Claims Can Proceed." Human Rights Concern Eritrea. November 21, 2017. HRC-Eritrea.org. http://hrc-eritrea.org/eritrea-canadian-appeal-court-affirms-eritreans-slavery-and-forced-labour-claims-can-proceed/

Hanna Petros "Solomon emotional testimony on 23 June 2016." *Asmarino Independent.* http://asmarino.com/articles/articles-video/4706-hanna-petros-solomon-emotional-testimony-on-23-june-2016.

Martin Plaut. "Who is Isaias Afwerki, Eritrea's Enigmatic Dictator?" *Newsweek.* November 1, 2016. http://www.newsweek.com/who-isaias-afwerki-eritreas-enigmatic-dictator-515761

Made in the USA
Middletown, DE
30 May 2019